FACING EVIL

Rudolf Steiner's sculpture The Representative of Humanity

FACING EVIL

and

THE GUARDIAN SPEAKS

Esoteric Lessons
of the First Class

Peter Selg

SteinerBooks | 2024

2024
STEINERBOOKS
an imprint of Anthroposophic Press, Inc.
834 Main Street, PO Box 358, Spencertown, New York 12165
www.steinerbooks.org

Translation by Jeff Martin

LIBRARY OF CONGRESS CONTROL NUMBER: 2023941176

ISBN: 978-1-62148-333-5

Printed in the United States of America
by Integrated Books International

Urkräfte haltet mich
Geister des Feuers befreiet mich
Geister des Lichtes erleuchtet mich
Dass ich greife nach Geistessein
Dass ich fühle die Seelenwesen
Dass ich schreite über Ungewissheiten
Dass ich stehe über Abgründen

Primal powers uphold me
Spirits of fire free me
Spirits of light illumine me
That I reach for spirit existence
That I feel the soul beings
That I step over uncertainties
That I stand over abysses

RUDOLF STEINER (for Ita Wegman)

Contents

Preface

The two essays in this book arose on the basis of lectures given to members of the School for Spiritual Science—the first on May 4, 2019, in Zürich, Switzerland, and the second on September 11, 2019, at the Goetheanum. They concern the confrontation with the forces of evil—both within the Class Lessons and outside of them—as well as the figure of the "Guardian of the Threshold," as a Michaelic teacher and companion of the human being on his path into the abysses of our time and into the crises of individual inner development. The Guardian—still too little understood today—is a helping spiritual being of great significance.

Other studies in this direction will follow in the future in order to deepen and internalize the work with the nineteen lessons of the First Class of the School for Spiritual Science within the community of School members. With the same goal in mind, a book was recently published (so far only in German): *Angeloi, Archangeloi, Archai. Der Mensch und die dritte Hierarchie. Zur Ersten Klasse der Freien Hochschule für Geisteswissenschaft* [Angeloi, Archangeloi, Archai. The human being and the third hierarchy. On the First Class of the School for Spiritual Science]. Moreover, the General Anthroposophical Section at the Goetheanum has established a free biannual newsletter for Class members, available in three languages. Here, shorter contributions from around the world are published, offering a deepened understanding of the Class lessons, the mantras, and the context in which they stand.

It is important to continually reflect upon Rudolf Steiner's conception of the School, including the relationship between the Class Lessons, the fields of human endeavor (Sections), and the practical work, as well as the relationship of the Anthroposophical Society to its own School. Essays that I recently wrote in connection with the centenary of the Christmas Conference are being published simultaneously with this book as *The Anthroposophical World Society and Its School for Spiritual Science*. Thanks to Jeff Martin, who translated the two essays in this book on the powers of evil and the Guardian of the Threshold.

Peter Selg
General Anthroposophical Section
Ita Wegman Institut
Dornach and Arlesheim
Michaelmas 2023

I

Facing Evil

Dear Class Members!

On November 3, 1917—in that "epoch-making year" of world history and of our present age[1]—Rudolf Steiner spoke powerfully about the "problem of evil" to be "solved" in our time, saying, among other things:

> We, the people of the fifth post-Atlantean age—and we are basically standing quite at the beginning of it (this fifth post-Atlantean age began in 1413, and such an epoch lasts 2,160 years)—have to solve, in the most comprehensive and vital way, what we can call the problem of evil. I ask you to consider this penetratingly. Evil, which will approach the people of the fifth post-Atlantean age in all possible forms, which will approach us in such a way that we will have to solve scientifically the nature and essence of evil, that we will have to come to terms in our loving and hating with everything that stems from evil, that we will have to fight, to wrestle with the opposition of evil against our will impulses—all this belongs to the fifth post-Atlantean age.[2]

At the beginning of the fifth post-Atlantean epoch, in the early fifteenth century, the supersensible Michael School was formed in the sphere of the spiritual sun, as Dr. Steiner described in the Karma Lectures, held after the Christmas Conference.[3] Michael taught in this school in "celestial solitude" before those who belong to him; he taught the teachings of the ancient mysteries, albeit in a transformed way, adapted and attuned to modernity. He prepared human souls associated with him, as well as higher beings belonging to his "stream" or "movement," for the coming times and their challenges. He gave them a "tremendous panorama of what is to happen," of "what has to happen when the new Michael Age begins."[4]

What began with the new Michael Age in 1879 was described by Rudolf Steiner in many lectures and texts, and I think it is well known to all of you. In the Karma Lectures, he also describes that among these events—and playing a central role in them—was the confrontation with evil, which, according to him, was already emerging at the beginning of the fifteenth century. Michael and his hosts observed from the sun region the formation of an ahrimanic counter-school in the depths of the earth, filled with demonic forces, which also prepared itself for the coming confrontations. At that time, the Michaelites perceived this only from cosmic heights and were not directly affected by it as observers. However, this changed dramatically when they began to incarnate at the end of the nineteenth and the beginning of the twentieth centuries. The ahrimanic forces from the depths of the earth are at work in the human organization too, and in the current Michael School, in the Esoteric Lessons of the First Class, it is described how the ahrimanic forces from the earth virtually force their way into our "bodily members." The students are asked to "feel" this happening, to visualize it perceptively. To let it happen unnoticed leads to a "darkening of the I," because through the forces rising up, a foreign determination of the will takes place, which is equal to a loss of self. ("You lose yourself in them,/If you entrust your will powerlessly/To their striving…"[5])

~

However, the central conflict since 1879 has not been, and is not primarily, about human will but about our thinking, about intelligence. In the wake of the Mystery of Golgotha, Michael has let go of the intelligence of the cosmos, the "cosmic intelligence" of the hierarchies, which he had "administered" through countless ages, successively placing it at the free disposal of earthly humanity. Rudolf Steiner reported in detail about this process in his Karma Lectures and in his *Anthroposophical Leading Thoughts* from the middle of 1924. Since the beginning of modern times, Ahriman and his followers—Ahriman and his "multitudes"—are in the process, within the earth sphere, of intercepting this intelligence coming "from above," so to speak. Ahriman wants to take up this intelligence, to bring it under his control, and to make it accessible to humanity in his own way. He now succeeds at this, and with far-reaching consequences, which Rudolf Steiner warned about:

> Intellectuality pours forth from Ahriman as a cold and freezing, soulless cosmic impulse. Those human beings who are taken hold of by this impulse bring forth the logic that seems to speak for itself alone, void of compassion and of love, which bears no evidence of a right, heartfelt, inner relationship of soul between the human being and what he thinks and speaks and does.…[6]
>
> All his thinking becomes an experience of the head; but this separates it from the experience of his own heart and the life of his own will, and blots out his own being. Man loses more and more of the true inner human

expression by becoming the expression of his own separate existence....[7]

This alienated intelligence, this ahrimanized thinking, no longer carries cosmic qualities or real spirituality. "Rejecting spiritual powers which/Before its life on earth / Kept it spiritually alive in spiritual fields"[8]—such thinking denies its own being and chooses death, the domain of Ahriman on earth. It is a "corpse" of actual thinking, only an "inheritance" of what was once living; it carries death in itself and causes death[9]—the kind of death caused by such thinking in the fields of natural science and technology, in the "weapons of mass destruction" and the death factories of the twentieth century, in the destructive technology of the present and near future. "The dead thinking of the nineteenth century has driven dead materialism to the surface of human civilization," says Rudolf Steiner in the Class Lessons.[10]

The "mighty vista" of the cosmic Michael School, the vista of "what is to happen," of "what has to happen when the new Michael Age begins," also speaks to the shadow side of the period beginning in 1879. To be an anthroposophist, Rudolf Steiner once emphasized, means to understand this struggle "at least to a certain degree."[11] And to be a Michaelite means even more than that—it means being prepared to "throw oneself into" this struggle so that intelligence can in turn be united with the Michael-being.[12] Thus, we arrive at the whole drama of the twentieth century.

~

At this point, I would like to relate a personal experience. In the last year of his life, Sergei O. Prokofieff asked me to read the manuscript of his second book on the Class Lessons, to which he wanted to give the title *The Esoteric Path through the Nineteen Class Lessons in the Light of the Supersensible Mystery of Golgotha and the Fifth Gospel.* However, he was uncertain whether he should really publish it or how it would be received and discussed. He asked me for a quick reading. Since I was on my way to a meeting in Berlin, I took the manuscript with me and spent my free hours in Berlin looking for a quiet place to read—I didn't want to read it in the city's subways or suburban trains.

My path finally led me to the Old Jewish Cemetery on Grosse Hamburger Strasse in Berlin-Mitte, probably not by chance. It has been the burial place of Berlin's Jews since 1672 and was desecrated by the Nazis in a cruel, unimaginable way. They destroyed the cemetery, leveled it, and dug a ditch that they secured with gravestones; and they did other equally cruel things in this place, out of cynicism and ice-cold hatred; then they designated the Jewish retirement home at the entrance of the cemetery, which dated back to 1844, as the main deportation center for Berlin Jews, from which they were "deported" to the Polish extermination camps. In this way, approximately 55,000 victims passed through the. historic site of the Old Jewish Cemetery or retirement home on Grosse Hamburger Strasse. Today, it is a quiet place of remembrance, with still a few old gravestones, including that of Moses Mendelssohn, the friend of Lessing and role model of Nathan the Wise; but one feels, or at least seems to feel, in the earth, in the soil, and in the nearby surroundings, what once went on there.

So, there I read the studies of Sergei O. Prokofieff about the first four Lessons, about the abyss and the "beasts," and about the spiritual background of what is developed in the Lessons, and I must say: the explosiveness and reality of the whole thing dawned on me only there, on those cemetery grounds that had witnessed such horror; or, let us say, a new dimension of the Class Lessons dawned on me. We hear in the Lessons the words, "You can, when death's power restrains you/Cramp the self in nothingness,"[13] and making the connection for the first time, there in Berlin while reading the words in Sergei's manuscript, I thought of how people died in the gas chambers, suffocating and "cramping" in a terrible way in the "nothingness" of the poisonous gas. And yet the quoted words concern rather the murderers, those whom the darkness "tempted" and who lost their "selves" in "matter"—and in the end, when the power of death "subdued" them, actually "cramped" their selves in the "nothingness." The I of their victims remained untouched, but the I of the murderers was completely darkened. The "selfhood delusion" belonged, in its luciferic quality, to German National Socialism, to the marches and uniforms, to the self-exaltation of the "elites," to the SA and SS, to the titles and intoxication. It led to "stifled selfhood," and finally to "murdered self-experience."[14]

The militant National Socialist, as an ahrimanized human being, served a real death movement and annihilation stream, and German National Socialism was such a movement—it held within itself the secrets of death *and* evil, the secrets of the fourth and fifth post-Atlantean cultural epochs.[15] The murderers in National Socialism—they were the ones who "unfolded their acts in death," "acted in death," "acted in nothingness," to use Rudolf Steiner's formulations in the fifth Class Lesson.

Perhaps you have the impression that I am portraying the whole thing a bit too pathetically and dramatically; but I would like to say from experience that the mantric words of the Class Lessons sound different in the wretched places of humanity, speak to us differently, have other overtones or undertones that we do not always hear *in the same way* in the therapy center of the Arlesheim Clinic—as a place for our Class Lessons—or in our Branch rooms. Likewise, the Consecration of the Human Being sounds different in Birkenau, next to the ruins of the gas chambers; the "presence of good" and many other such words, sound different to us there. And I think the whole thing concerns us *as members of the Michael School*, as those who want to "throw themselves into the struggle," as Rudolf Steiner said.

Individual anthroposophists also participated the misery of which I have just spoken—one of many in the twentieth century. They belonged to it, as victims *and* perpetrators. You may know about the victimization of people like Maria Darmstädter and Viktor Ullmann, who belong to us, but you may also know about Sigmund Rascher, who was a member of the Anthroposophical Society, a coworker in the Dornach Glass House, and a participant in Rudolf Steiner's "Young Doctors" courses. He, Sigmund Rascher, as an SS doctor, not only made the cruelest human experiments in the Dachau concentration camp but also developed the cyanide capsules that the top SS elite (people like Heinrich Himmler) carried in their mouths and only had to chew in case of capture, so as not to fall into the hands of justice. Himmler died this way—by ingesting hydrocyanic acid.[16] Rascher developed the capsules and tried them out on prisoners in Dachau. I wonder if he knew what

Rudolf Steiner said about the afterlife consequences of
death by hydrocyanic acid?[17]

Regardless, Sigmund Rascher worked in the midst of an
ahrimanic death zone, as an anthroposophist who had to
know what he was doing, which forces and powers he served.
He was completely addicted to Heinrich Himmler and the
National Socialist death and extermination movement—not
only outwardly but also in his innermost being; this is not
an excuse, but rather a judgment of being. "You can, if darkness entices you/Lose the self in matter."... "Delusion of
selfhood—stifled selfhood—murdered selfhood...."

~

Now, I would like to move on from such extreme examples,
but it seemed to me important to point out these aspects of
some Class mantras, some "mantric thoughts," as a world-
historical example from the recent past, from the fight of
Michael with the terrible power of Ahriman. The fact that
we are talking about this here today, two weeks after Easter,
seems to me to be essential. During Passiontide, up to and
including Holy Saturday, the Consecration of the Human
Being speaks of the "sting of evil" in the heart of earthly
humanity, and also of the "tempting power" and the weakness of humanity. The I lying on the ground and lamenting, spoken of in the cultus, resonates intimately in the Old
Jewish Cemetery in Grosse Hamburger Strasse, but also in
our own day, in the face of overwhelming powers of chaos
and destruction in the world—the I lying on the ground,
lamenting, asking to be raised—"Raise it, Spirit/Of the
world afar/And of the earth near...."[18] Then follows, sea-
sonally and cultically, the resurrection event, the healing of
the I "in the depths of the soul." The cultic words: "There

lives the soul/That was dead/There shines the I/That was dark/There works the spirit/That was sealed"[19] can speak to us intimately as members of the Esoteric School of the Goetheanum, the Michael School. Our esoteric path is, after all, centered on the task of becoming bright and "luminous" in the I, in the connection of the I with an illuminating, brightening spiritual world that is initially quite dark to us. "There shines the I/That was dark/There works the spirit/That was sealed...."

And today, on this fourth day of May, we are within the forty days between Easter and the Ascension, during which the Risen Christ took His disciples into what Rudolf Steiner literally called "esoteric schooling."[20] He instructed them—Dr. Steiner spoke of the "teachings of the Risen One"—in His spiritual body, walking with them. Luke's Acts of the Apostles says:

> By many manifestations of his being, he had shown himself as the victor over death after his passion. For forty days he revealed himself to their seeing souls and spoke to them of the mysteries of the Kingdom of God. (Acts 1:3)[21]

Accordingly, not only were there "many manifestations" of the Risen Christ, but there was a form of continuous presence ("for forty days") and ongoing teaching ("he...spoke to them of the mysteries of the Kingdom of God"), a teaching which, however, was not made known by the four evangelists. The disciples perceived, as Rudolf Steiner emphasized, the Christ in his etheric body, which was "condensed" to visibility. In this etheric body, he remained united with them for forty days after Easter. The "power of the disciples being together with the Christ" persisted and reached a new form and quality. "For forty days in a row the disciples were clear about it: the Christ is still there...."[22] But this existence and this kind of presence had in fact, as Rudolf Steiner described in his explanations of the Acts of the Apostles, the character of a "teaching," even of an "esoteric schooling." Although the Christ-being's effect on the disciples at this time took place mainly in the subconscious regions of their souls, he spoke "with them"—especially about his experiences in overcoming death on earth and thereby also Ahriman, with whom he had fought for three days in his kingdom ("then he overcame death after three days...."[23]).

The Christ-being had descended to earth to have *this* experience, the experience of the ahrimanized earth-death and its overcoming. For the sake of this experience, which had to be shared, Christ had come and had become human. This now became a teaching, an "esoteric schooling," which the disciples internalized—"Thus thinks in us Christ's suffering and death/his resurrection...."[24] For it was the task of the disciples "to teach and heal" in the future—i.e., to spread a new human and cosmic picture in the light of the Golgotha event and to work therapeutically.[25] For this, they needed a spiritual schooling. This schooling had to be not only about their personal I, their personal salvation, but also about their task or about the ability to fulfill this task—"so that the good may exist."[26] It was not only about a form of personal, individual further development, but about the "continuation of man's being"—thus, the renewed creed of original Christianity.[27]

I think it is clear to many of us that the Esoteric School of the Goetheanum, our Michael School, is also about nothing else. In this school and through its schooling, people are to be prepared and enabled to fulfill tasks in the world, "teaching and healing," in the triumphant confrontation with the "prince of this world," with the forces of decline and destruction. Recently, I have repeatedly tried to point out, both in lectures and in writing, that Rudolf Steiner recognized not only a "personal membership" in the School for Spiritual Science of the Goetheanum, but also a "professional membership"—and included in it not only the doctors but also all the teachers of the Stuttgart Waldorf School and all the priests of the Christian Community; and he would certainly have done the same in the future with other professional groups and practical communities, if they had been formed, with farmers, artists, natural scientists, economists, etc.[28] All these people need an inner armor to be able to work and exist in the world with their spiritual-social work, to be able to "work" in this ahrimanized world, as it is said in the Children's Service of the Christian Community. The Michaelites need "to reflect on the needs of earth," "on everything that suffers on earth" and that must be grasped in all its gravity; they need a Franciscan "love for earth values" (for "earth weaving in forms and shapes"), and they need a "spirit-resulting earth will"[29] in order to be able to work for the forces of resurrection in the individual fields of civilization, in the sense of the Goetheanum, in the School for Spiritual Science, in the age of Michael.

Rudolf Steiner's young listeners in the year 1924 went out with their "healing work" into a difficult time; the history of the twentieth century includes 187 million violent deaths, immeasurable abysses and destructions that had never before been seen in human history. It actually became an epoch in which evil gained a whole new power on earth, and we are still living in the middle of this epoch. "Humanity has a strong obsession with the forces of evil, with the love of evil," emphasized Rudolf Steiner,[30] and this is still true. From this point of view, it is a good, a right, and important coincidence that today, barely two weeks after Easter Sunday, within the forty days, we are taking up this theme and putting it at the center of our meeting for one evening, even if only in outline. The Michaelic struggle in which we stand, and should stand, and indeed must stand as anthroposophists, has essentially to do with this theme; and it begins with the fact that we meet the "cold death" in thinking with a "counterforce" or begin "to call forth in thought the living spirit from inner strength."[31] This is, in a certain way, how anthroposophy began, as we can see in detail by studying its historical development—beginning with Rudolf Steiner's first writings.[32]

~

In this struggle, however, we are lost as single individuals, completely lost—we must admit that; only in community do we have even the slightest chance of being able to fortify and support ourselves within this battle. It seems to me very important in this context to understand that the Esoteric School of the Goetheanum, the Michael School— in addition to being a non-personal matter with a professional aspect—is a deeply communal matter. It is—at least *also*—about self-knowledge in the community and about self-knowledge for a community, for the formation of a Michael or Michaelite community after the Christmas Conference. And here I would like to say: what a different Anthroposophical Society and community we would have if this esoteric schooling in the confrontation with evil had really become fruitful, had, in the last ninety-five years, really reached the goal set in 1924!

Let us just survey the history of our own Society: How many problems there have been since 1902 because individual anthroposophists did not notice, or did not want to notice, when the semblance of light thought itself in them ("when the semblance of light thinks itself in you"), where they spread "untrue spiritual life" and got entangled in the "delusion of selfhood," in the luciferically inspired fantasies of occultism.[33] They may not have noticed it themselves—and neither did many other anthroposophists and Class members, who rather followed these persons in droves and were not able to distinguish between "being" and "semblance," which weakened the Society and community in the long run. ("One must acquire a whole new ability to distinguish between reality and illusion."[34]) And on the other, opposite side, we have the ahrimanized intellectuality in dealing with anthroposophy, and by no means only in the non-anthroposophical "outside world," among the opponents of anthroposophy, with their doubt, ridicule, hatred, and fear, but also internally, in our midst and in no small measure.

And further: How many problems there were and are in the Anthroposophical Society and community—also in the School for Spiritual Science community—because the Christian middle ground of feeling was not found, the middle ground between the tempting poles of warmth and coldness, between the I-less devotion borne by warmth or heat ("the wafting-away of the self in spiritual pleasure") and the distanced antipathy, hardening in coldness.[35] On November 3, 1917, Rudolf Steiner said, with total clarity, that the problem of evil, which we have to solve, also concerns our innermost selves ("that we [human beings, and therefore anthroposo-phists] will have to come to terms in our loving and hating with everything that stems from evil..."). In our very own "loving and hating," we, too—as anthroposophists and Class members—carry an "unhealthy feeling" within us; in *our* feeling, too, the ahrimanic spirit "rummages in the unconscious," as Rudolf Steiner elaborated: "And all our prejudices of feeling are colored by ahrimanic influences, ahrimanic impulses within us."[36]

And finally, where would the Anthroposophical Society, where would the Goetheanum and its School for Spiritual Science stand nearly one hundred years after the Christmas Conference if we had found the balance in our will between the poles of excessive life, the seductive "spiritual power" that is close to megalomania, to self-overestimation, self-conceit, also in institutional terms, and suicidal resignation, withdrawal or relinquishment, a form of "death power"?[37] According to Rudolf Steiner, the human being of our epoch has to wrestle "with the resistances of evil against the impulses of the will"—we all have it, our Society and community. In our will, too, we find astonishing tendencies toward evil, toward that which is "lowly" in our beingness and acts powerfully:

> Those who really meditate honestly will see what urges actually live in their souls, what all they are actually capable of. There, already, the lower human nature appears powerfully before the inner vision of the soul.[38]

Where would we stand today as individuals and as a Society and community if only we had fully understood and implemented the first six Lessons of the First Class in which the deviations of evil are comprehensively described? Where would we be in our lives and in our anthroposophical work? In our circles, there is often the thought, and sometimes speculation, about a Second and Third Class; would we not rather have the task of internalizing through "thorough practice" [*durchzuüben*] (R. Steiner) at least *the first six Lessons* of the First Class in order to be able to become other people and other Michaelites in a community—an *effective* community?

What can we do so that we can still succeed in this in the future? Can we still achieve this future? Michael, who wants to work for the "salvation of mankind,"[39] needs helpers, coworkers, many coworkers—but they must be able to work together in their struggle in the world. They must be able to work together not only within their internal meetings, committees, conferences, and general assemblies, but in a united struggle in the world. What prevents us from doing this, however, is evil, yes, indeed—the "thorn" in our heart and our weakness, which is subject to the tempting power, in the spheres of thinking, feeling, and willing, as has just been said. We must take upon ourselves the "inner drama of self-knowledge"[40] and persist, not constantly complain about obstacles and evil powers in the "outside world"; we cannot perform "works" of supreme importance, but we can "conquer sin"[41]—or at least set out on the way to do so, in the "purification" or "metamorphosis" of our own beings,[42] "striving for salvation." For we all have the "forces for something better" in us, even if, at times, that is all we have, as Friedrich Schiller wrote: "I feel that in some hours there is nothing left in me but the forces for something better."[43] What counts, however, is the conscious will and determination to want to "don a completely new person," to quote Schiller again,[44] individually and as a prerequisite for new community:

> Serious, good will is the greatest, the most beautiful qual-
> ity of the spirit. Success lies in a higher invisible hand.
> Only intention gives value to our efforts.[45]

~

I think that younger people of another generation will come in the future—and to some extent are already here—who will see this social-spiritual task clearly and approach it with different inner preconditions, of that I am certain, also with regard to the esoteric schooling of the First Class. However, they are faced with a great task in this respect because the Class Lessons presuppose, in a certain respect, a knowledge of anthroposophy as a science of ideas, and only under certain conditions is it correct to begin with the Class Lessons, for this step is not without its accompanying dangers. Why? Why did Rudolf Steiner give a guideline that requires Society membership and about two years of study-ing the ideas of anthroposophy as prerequisites for Class participation? Why did he speak of a "preparation through general anthroposophy"?[46]

The Esoteric Lessons are not about ideas but—radically speaking—about beings, about their appearance and pres-ence in a direct and immediate sense. The Class Lessons, if they are really held in their esoteric power and greatness, create this presence of the concretely spiritual, of concrete spiritual immanence. One can experience this as a gift and grace, as something blissful. But it can also become too much, especially where it is about the abysses and abysmal beings, about "beasts" rising from the soul and about other things. And here it is, I think, helpful, meaningful, and instructive to have an understanding of Rudolf Steiner's differentiated teaching about the beings who are active here—indeed, this is not only a "good thing," it is unconditionally self-preserving and health-preserving. We are able not only to overtax people with the Class Lessons as esoteric actions, but also bring them into distress, into distress of understanding and subsequently also into distress of the soul. This has happened in the past. It is—to give only one example—infinitely important to understand that the three "beasts" already appearing in the First Lesson are not primarily a result of individual misbehavior, of one's own wickedness, weakness, and aberration, of one's own fall and decay, but an expression of the human situation in which we, as contemporaries, have a share. Rudolf Steiner speaks about this briefly in the course of the First Lesson, and the mantric wording names this explicitly ("Your epoch has placed them [the beasts] in you/As enemies of knowledge"[47]); the whole situation has a much broader, world-historical background, which is not and cannot be spoken of in detail in the Class Lesson itself; it must be an esoteric lesson and not an instructional lecture.

Many other things, too, I think, must be understood anthroposophically in a fundamental way before, as in the Class Lessons, they are allowed to have an essential effect on one and then be meditated on, inwardly enlivened and deepened. This seems to me of great importance with regard to the teaching of evil, and also in other areas. We all know that we can freely confront the anthroposophical teaching of ideas, freely confront it in our own experience. ("One must be able to confront the idea, experiencing it; *otherwise,* one falls into bondage to it," Rudolf Steiner famously wrote in the appendix to his *Philosophy of Spiritual Activity.*[48])

In an esoteric lesson, we are not "unfree" from the outset; nevertheless, the situation is completely different, as everyone knows who has participated, and is participating, in the actual enactment of the Michael School.

In view of this, I would like to say in this lecture, at this point, at least a few brief words about Rudolf Steiner's descriptions of the adversarial powers, including Ahriman, in world creation, which belong to the background and overall context of the relevant passages of the Class Lessons. It seems to me important, indeed indispensable, that new Class members know about these connections and spiritual-scientific perspectives, at least in outline. We cannot assume knowledge of the entire Collected Works in them or in us, and will be less and less able to do so in the future. But the longing to listen to the Esoteric Lessons and to work with them inwardly will grow, of that I am sure, because they are appropriate and necessary for the times we live in, especially for the successful confrontation with evil. The longing for them is growing and will continue to grow, indeed incomparably faster and more intensively than for the study of anthroposophical spiritual science as such, as a teaching of ideas in the sense mentioned above.

~

In his spiritual-scientific lectures and writings, Rudolf Steiner has described a differentiated intervention of powers in the development of humankind on earth—in the soul body by Lucifer, in the life body by Ahriman, and in the physical body by the asuras, who appeared last in human evolution and are becoming more and more powerful. They take aim not only at the physical body but at the same time also at human I-consciousness—indeed, at the I itself.[49]

According to Steiner, Lucifer and his hosts already approached the human organization at the end of the Lemurian epoch. At this vulnerable point in time, when humanity slowly became ripe to receive the seed of the I, the human being in his astral body was exposed to Lucifer's influences. From then on, according to Rudolf Steiner, Lucifer made himself felt and occasioned the appearance of instincts and passions, whereby humanity's perception of the spiritual world and of spiritual beings began to darken. This eclipse of the spiritual world appears at the beginning of the Class Lessons; this eclipse began in very ancient times, in that time which various myths describe as the loss of the state of innocence and purity, as the expulsion from the light of "paradise" (or the paradisal land of innocence) into the sense world, which became the focus.

> If the luciferic beings had not come, human beings would have remained in a state of perpetually longing for their home, for the spiritual realms from which they descended. They would not have found pleasure in what surrounded them on earth; they could not possibly have been interested in earthly impressions. They came to this interest, to this desire for earthly impressions, through the luciferic spirits. They have forced humans into the earthly sphere by permeating their innermost beings, their astral bodies.[50]

Through this impregnation, we human beings entered the physical world early or prematurely and developed a relative autonomy, following our own impulses and imagining ourselves to be "free" in them. We learned to perceive the sense world in material form with our increasingly dense physical body. Thus, we—from the middle of Atlantis—became more and more accessible to the unremitting influences of Ahriman—indeed, we surrendered to them. Finally, it was Ahriman who led us completely down into the physical-sensory world and weakened our perceptive and conceptual capacity with regard to spiritual experience, which, according to Rudolf Steiner, at the same time allowed deception, error, and evil to enter into the evolution of humanity—or rather allowed humanity to make such phenomena possible: "If humans would see the spiritual in every stone, in every plant, and in every animal, they would never have fallen into error and thus into evil, but human beings, if solely the progressing spirits had acted upon them, would have remained preserved from those illusions to which they must always succumb if they rely only on the testimony of the sense world."[51]

Since the middle of Atlantis, Ahriman has been connected with humanity and earth evolution, literally; for he maintains the center of his activity directly within a layer of the earth. He influenced—and influences—human life in momentous ways between birth and death, but also after death; this has been going on for a very long time. The difficulties of the inner orientation of the dead in the world of the spirit, the "agonies of not understanding" are spoken of in various places in the esoteric Class Lessons (and of the helping power of esoteric schooling in this situation: "That souls remain alive when they pass through the gate of death, for this there are esoteric schools..."[52]). According to Rudolf Steiner, it was and is especially the ahrimanic influence that underlies the post-mortem loneliness and helplessness of human souls—a development that had already taken on a threatening dynamic many millennia ago, before the Mystery of Golgotha provided a first remedy. "In death he became the helper of the souls of the dead who had lost their divine being...."[53] Describing the situation, Rudolf Steiner said:

> Souls felt lonely and in dark surroundings in the spiritual world before the event of Golgotha occurred. At that time, the spiritual world was not transparent in all its luminous clarity for those who, coming through the gate of death, stepped into it. All felt alone, pushed back into themselves, as if a wall had been erected between themselves and other souls. And this would have become stronger and stronger. Souls would have hardened in their I, souls would have been completely turned back on themselves, none would have found the bridge to the other. People would have then been incarnated again, and if egoism was already very great before, it would have become more tremendous with each new incarnation.
>
> The whole of earth existence would have made the human being more and more the wildest egoist. There would have been no prospect of a brotherhood, an inner harmony of souls, ever coming about on the earthly plane; for with each passage through the spiritual realm, stronger influences would have entered the I.[54]

Through Golgotha, this situation changed decisively. I do not wish to discuss this further at the moment. Instead, I would like to emphasize that humanity's after-death situation again became seriously complicated and worsened during the nineteenth century, which witnessed the culmination of materialism. Human souls became increasingly impregnated in their thinking, feeling, and willing by the effects of materialism on the living environment, and they carried the results of this soul-deformation into the after-death world of spirit (and into the etheric surroundings of the earth) with serious consequences.[55]

Ahriman is powerful and becoming more and more powerful. He not only appropriates cosmic intelligence in a cold and soulless manner, passing it on to us, who may become slaves to ahrimanized cognition and abstraction, but he also exerts his influence on spiritually striving souls, leading them into deceptions and illusions, generating abnormal dispositions, states, and perceptions permeated with egoism and the will to power—and much more. "Protection in the world against the influence of Ahriman will come less and less from outside the forces emanating from the Christ mystery," Rudolf Steiner emphasized on January 1, 1909, in Berlin,[56] in his first extensive lecture on Lucifer *and* Ahriman, on the double figure of evil of which he was to speak frequently from that time on. Only three weeks later, in writing and in lectures, he dealt for the first time in detail with the next category of evil, discussing the asuras. ("The Deed of Christ and the Adversary Powers of Lucifer, Ahriman, and the Asuras," Berlin, March 22, 1909[57])—beings from the hierarchy of the archai, spiritually superior to Ahriman and Lucifer (who are retarded archangeloi and angeloi), who already veered off from the divine line of creation of Earth and humanity on Old Saturn: "The asuras will develop evil with a much more intense force than even the satanic powers of the Atlantean or even the luciferic spirits of Lemurian times."[58] Describing not only a further intensification of evil but an entirely new quality that no longer serves human development, Steiner explained:

> The evil that the luciferic spirits brought to humanity at the same time as the benefit of freedom—all this we will completely cast off in the course of Earth evolution. The evil brought by the ahrimanic spirits can be cast off through the course of karmic law. But the evil brought

by the asuric powers cannot be expiated in such a way. Whereas the good spirits have given us pain and suffering, sickness and death, so that we can develop upward in spite of the possibility of evil, whereas the good spirits have given the possibility of karma to counterbalance the ahrimanic powers and to make up for error, this will not be so easy in relation to the asuric spirits as earthly evolution progresses. For these asuric spirits will cause what they seize—and this is, after all, the human being's deepest inner being, the consciousness soul with the I—to be united with the sensuality of the earth. They will tear out the I, piece by piece. In the same measure as the asuric spirits settle in the consciousness soul, in the same measure human beings must leave behind pieces of their existence on earth. That which has fallen to the asuric powers will be irretrievably lost. Not that the whole human being has to fall prey to them, but pieces will be cut out of the human spirit by the asuric powers.

These asuric powers announce themselves in our age through the prevailing spirit, which we could call the spirit of mere life in sensuality and of forgetting all real spiritual beings and spiritual worlds. One could say that today the temptation of the asuras remains somewhat theoretical. Today they often deceive us that our I is just the result of the mere physical world. Today they seduce us to a kind of theoretical materialism. But in the further course of evolution—and this is announced by the wild passions of sensuality that descend more and more upon the earth—they will darken the human being's view of spiritual beings and spiritual powers. The human being will know nothing and will want to know nothing of a spiritual world. More and more, it will be taught that the highest human moral ideas are only higher forms of animal instincts; it will be taught that human thinking is only a transformation of what the animal also has; it will be taught that human beings are not only related to animals according to their form, but

that humanity is also descended from the animal according to their whole being, and people will take this view
seriously and live in this way.[59]

This attack aims without any doubt at the I and at
that "higher I" which is attainable for us precisely in our
specifically human capacity—in the transcendence of the
sensory-physical world. This path concerns attaining this
higher I, which remains prenatally in the spiritual world
and accompanies our earthly path, more than determining
it, but also appears in outstanding moments of existence
and is found again at death. It concerns attaining the higher
I in a central way on the path of esoteric schooling within
the Michael School. Out of the higher I-forces, on the basis
of a developed consciousness soul, the Dornach School for
Spiritual Science was to become effective in civilization.[60]
Against this stand not only Lucifer and Ahriman, but also
the asuras, who want to promote a whole other "culture"
and are already far advanced in this, proceeding extraordi-
narily successfully. In this direction, as Rudolf Steiner indi-
cated, they are in the service of Sorat, the actual cosmic
opponent of the Christ-being, the "true I" and the spiritual
sun-principle. Sorat fights I-ness as such, not only the individual I in its manifestation and becoming, but the possibility of the I in general. Lucifer, Ahriman, and the asuras
work for him through their influences on the astral body
(Lucifer), the etheric body (Ahriman), and the physical
body (asuras). They corrupt I-ness, undermining its becoming and being—*through* the lifestyle, life-attitude, and
life-perception to which they seduce humanity, a life- and
self-perception that amounts to a progressive self-alienation
and self-annihilation. "Most people would be more easily

brought to think of themselves as a piece of lava on the moon than as an I," Fichte wrote in a footnote to his *Wissenschaftslehre* already more than two hundred years ago.[61] But this problem increases dramatically in the age of the asuras; it is systematically sharpened by them and becomes a serious existential problem for humanity on Earth.

~

Then why, it was asked again and again in view of this scenario of evil, do the Esoteric Lessons after the Christmas meeting "only" speak of Lucifer and Ahriman, but not of the asuras and of Sorat? And why do the higher and incomparably more dangerous powers of evil not appear in Rudolf Steiner's *Mystery Dramas*? And why not in the sculpture of the Representative of Humanity in the midst of the powers of evil, which again include only Lucifer and Ahriman? The answer is not simple. It can be said with good reason that Steiner was often very secretive, a "great silence"—despite the thousands of lectures and his many books—and only then spoke about something in front of actual people, in a concrete context, when he considered it useful. He once emphasized:

> I have no other aspiration than this: To explore what is possible for me to communicate from supersensible worlds in cognitive form with the right sense of responsibility before the present science, the present humanity. I either bring forward what I myself consider appropriate for present humanity, in its spiritual state of maturity, or those things for which individual groups of people first acquire the maturity in an (esoteric) preparatory schooling.[62]

Furthermore, I think that his concentration on Lucifer and Ahriman was meaningful and necessary, and still is to a large extent today. Dealing with them, their influences and forces, is of primary and urgent importance to us because the successful temptation by Lucifer and Ahriman is the necessary precondition for the much broader activity of the asuras and Sorat. The latter need the preliminary work, the distraction and the alienation of the truly human by Lucifer and Ahriman; if this alienation fails, the Asura and Sorat powers have no real access to humanity. How intensively Rudolf Steiner wrote about Ahriman, and about the Michaelic confrontation with him, right up until his last days on earth!

Moreover, in our context, which is a human *and* historical one, it has to be considered that Lucifer and Ahriman belong to the development of humanity on earth. They harbor an I in their being, and they have exercised their influence since individuals incarnated on earth and have had individual destinies. They belong to these destinies, as Steiner explained again and again. He once emphasized:

> For the good of humanity, therefore, certain Mights had to receive adverse commands. They were not evil to begin with—one need not regard them as evil forces—rather one could say that they sacrificed themselves in order to place an obstacle in the path of development. These Mights may, therefore, be called the "Gods of Hindrance," or "Gods of Impediment" in the broadest sense of the word. These are gods of obstructions or hindrances that have been placed along the path of development; and ever since that moment, the possibility was created for everything that was to be accomplished in the future. These countermanded dynamis were not yet evil in themselves; on the contrary, by running up against the normal course of development, they were the great promoters of evolution. Nevertheless, they were the originators of evil because, out of the storms they produced, evil gradually arose.[63]

The asuras and Sorat, for their part, have never been "promoting" powers of human development, and they never will be; they have also not "sacrificed" themselves—especially not Sorat—and are definitely *not* "gods of hindrances and obstacles" in the service of our becoming; they rather aim at destruction and annihilation. We all know from anthroposophical teachings, but also from our own respective lives, what we actually owe to the (luciferic-ahrimanic) possibilities of error, seduction, and evil; we know what significance it had and has in our lives to be able to rise above error and evil by our own power. What we owe to Lucifer and Ahriman is the possibility of going astray *and* the power to resist. They, Lucifer and Ahriman, belong to our path of development, to the path of the I, thus also to the Michael School. We owe them ultimately the path to freedom, a freedom which even the highest hierarchies do not have, "cannot reach from themselves," as Rudolf Steiner emphasized. Thus, the seraphim carry out, as it were, divine "orders," from their direct contemplation of the Godhead, the Trinity. Freedom, according to Steiner, begins only within the realm of the angels and comes to the right formation only with the human being, and this thanks to Lucifer and Ahriman:

> Freedom can arise only through the fact that the human being himself furnishes the highest content of his Earth-I. The I that the human being would have if all the goals were given to him at the end of Earth evolution cannot be free; for it would have been decided from the beginning to let all the fruits of Earth evolution flow into human beings. The human being could become free only by adding to this I another I capable of error, which is able to swing ever and again to the side of good and to the side of evil and which can strive upward ever and again to the content of

Earth evolution. The lower I had to be given to the human being by Lucifer so that the human being can, as his very own deed, work his way up to the higher I.[64]

Also our passions, which humanity owes to the luciferic and ahrimanic influence on our being, belong to our human dignity and self-determination, to our zeal and fire, and can become, through further development, the "fire of love creative of being," *provided* that we want this and actually strive for it in the pursuit of our inner schooling.

Lucifer and Ahriman, according to Rudolf Steiner, do not have to be designated from the outset as "evil powers" but are actually active in service of the development of humanity and thus also of the work of the gods—up to a certain limit. They "sacrificed" themselves, dropped out of their previous development, remained, according to Steiner, behind or "at a standstill" and cannot develop further by their own power. They are virtually imprisoned in their being and realm, as we see vividly expressed in the Representative of Humanity. The character of Strader in the *Mystery Dramas* almost feels pity for Ahriman. ("In your rough words there is the sound of pain/in you; and they cause pain in me as well./I must lament—beholding you—can only weep."[65])

The "fully conscious struggle against the evil appearing in the development of humanity," of which Rudolf Steiner spoke as the task of our epoch, is not a campaign of annihilation; with regard to Lucifer and Ahriman, they do not strive for humanity's extinction but rather for our overcoming. In the future, they must withdraw to the place of their rightful activity—but for this, they must first of all be stopped in their activity and limited:

There is only one power from which Lucifer withdraws: morality. This is something that burns Lucifer like the most terrible fire. And there is no other means by which to counteract Ahriman than judgment and discernment schooled in spiritual science. For what we acquire on earth as healthy powers of judgment is something that Ahriman flees from terribly. There is essentially nothing toward which he has a greater aversion than what we acquire through a healthy schooling of our I-consciousness.[66]

Judgment, discernment, and morality are schooled on the anthroposophical path of development, including in the First Class. By recognizing evil and trying to oppose it with good, we limit its effectiveness. With regard to Lucifer and Ahriman, it seems essential that we develop a certain dimension and breadth—breadth of way and being—toward them. It is a matter of understanding that the evil represented by Lucifer and Ahriman is a part of our world and of our self, our resistance and our corrective, through which we can and must grow, which we have to embrace courageously if we want to transform ourselves and move forward. In the face of the asuras and Sorat, this is no longer possible in this form—and the ahrimanic activity of the twentieth century passes over, blurring boundaries, into the territory of these darker powers.

Rudolf Steiner emphasized in 1917 that we must strive to follow the contemporary phenomena of evil "with a seeing eye."[67] He elaborated on this in an innovative way in his anthroposophical lectures. In particular, his accounts of the "epoch-making year" 1917 are, in my opinion, still worth very close reading.[68] It seems important to me to note what Dr. Steiner was already doing for the spiritualization of humanity and the counteracting of evil through his teaching of anthroposophical ideas. In 1917, he described for the first time what happens to people who die with a materialistic frame of mind—i.e., people who were unable to gain any other perspectives, not always because they did not want to but often because none were available to them in the surrounding culture. After death, they become servants of destructive processes that are initiated by powers of the cosmos, by "forces of destruction in the universe," which become active on earth. This terrible connection, which Steiner even explained publicly in a lecture in Berne in 1917,[69] must certainly be kept in mind when one asks what is to be done in this respect on the part of anthroposophy.

> In practice, this means we are challenged to do everything we can to encourage spiritual life as the only way of freeing future humanity from those destructive forces. It has to be clearly understood, of course, that this was different in the past, when the fact that an age of materialism must inevitably summon up an age of wars and devastation did not hold true to the same degree. It will, however, hold true in future.[70]

But let us return, after this exploration of various ideas, to the Class Lessons themselves, which promote the "spiritual life" in their own way.

~

You all know that the forces and powers of evil have a prominent place in the first third of the path through the nineteen Class Lessons, in Lessons One through Six. It is no accident that the Seventh Lesson says: "Enter/The gate is open/You will become/A true human being."[71] But *before that* comes the confrontation with evil. We can also say: If we do not manage to guide this confrontation positively, to pass through it, indeed, to triumph in it—the confrontation with the "dark earth realm," with the abyss and the beings of the abyss, the "beasts," our own animality—if we do not succeed in this, no door opens and we do not become a "true human being." We can still hear or read the rest of the Lessons, but they remain only theory—and they are in this case, in a certain sense, not meant for us. If the darkness of the earth "extinguishes" the I, then this I does not go further, it cannot go further, and no gate opens into that world of light in which it must itself shine. We must rediscover and "re-cognize" the "light of our own human self," as Rudolf Steiner said in the Class Lessons.[72]

And the nature of the abyss *in us* is articulated quite clearly and comprehensibly on this first part of the path. "Dead thinking" does not only exist within a certain manifestation of modern natural science and its technology but also within us. Within us, there is "dead thinking," a "corpse" in the "grave of our own head, our own brain,"—dead thinking even in dealing with anthroposophy, which has to be recognized, has to be recognized in ourselves.

When Ita Wegman asked the emaciated and weakening Rudolf Steiner in September 1924—in the midst of his five parallel courses in Dornach—to urgently reduce the number of lectures for reasons of health, she received not only a refusal but also a remarkable justification: "These lectures do not tire me at all, these lectures keep me healthy," he said, "what tires is the dead thoughts that approach one; it is the lack of understanding, the non-understanding of people which paralyzes one."[73] Even in dealing with anthroposophy, "dead," self-denying thinking is possible, thinking or imagination that is not infused with resurrection forces, not infused with life but its opposite: "Rejecting spiritual powers which/Before its life on earth/Kept it spiritually alive in spiritual fields"—although anthroposophy's content is precisely about these "spiritual powers."

The process is tragic, and we are familiar with this process, when we examine it more closely, not only in others but first and foremost in ourselves. It is *we* whose thinking—in spite of anthroposophy and even in our work with anthroposophy—does not have the necessary vitality but tends toward dead abstraction, toward the shadowy and the theoretical, toward schema and compulsion, toward assertive quotation, dogma, and opinions, in short: toward death. Rudolf Steiner already stated "that in the minds of many, anthroposophy is to a certain extent indistinguishable from external science...."[74] The souls and spirits of the supersensible world cannot incline to such thinking— here Michael does not set up his "new abode" in the heart. "When we grasp theoretical ideas, a universe dies within those ideas," said Steiner.[75] And Friedrich Schiller says: "Out of life/Two paths are open to you:/One leads to the ideal,/The other to death."[76]

But, in addition, our feeling is mentioned, which is by no means always filled with the "spiritual content" of the luminous "spiritual sun power" that shone into it prenatally, or rather pre-conceptually. In daily life, our life of feeling is often narrow in scope, even if we, with the help of anthroposophy, are given a great, luminous content "in earth-being," which carries, sustains, and illuminates us; many of us at least suspect what would have become of us in our feeling souls *without* anthroposophy in the twentieth century. The "emptiness of the soul" and the experience of meaninglessness, of suicidal nothingness was not alien to many anthroposophists before their encounter with Michaelic spiritual science—their own souls harassed and "hollowed out" by the nihilism of the present. The "emptiness of soul" can be found not only in space but also in human beings themselves as the triumph of an evil "counterforce," as the triumph of the "anti-Michael demons.... Keep strong my soul that in the time to come it die not," as it says in the renewed Christian cultus[77]—and this potential death of the soul is a reality, also within the anthroposophical context, as the historical crises within our community show us.[78]

And finally: we know of even the alienated body, the body alienated from the soul and the self, which is spoken of at the beginning of the schooling of the Michael School. Not only are we stunned by the evidence of bodily exploitation under National Socialism, by the mountains of hair in the collections of the Auschwitz "main camp" in Block 4, hair cut off from the victims in order to be sold to German textile and carpet factories for fifty Pfennigs a kilo, but we are also stunned by the "achievements" of modern body-technology (including genetic engineering): strategies to optimize what is no longer considered to be the supporting, even biography-bearing, body of a human being—the expression of his or her selfhood—but something completely different, the product of an "anti-aging medicine" or some other technological procedure for physical performance enhancement or other changes in human life.[79] In 1917, Rudolf Steiner spoke for the first time about coming "vaccinations" against spiritual tendencies of the soul and outlined a horrifying panorama of the future in this respect:

In addition to the various remedies, to the bodily remedies, that exist today, there will be a series of others that will be intended to treat those who speak of something as fantastical as spirit and soul; they will be cured, they will be given medicines so that they no longer speak of spirit and soul. The spirit needed merely to be abolished; the soul can be driven out of people only by treating the body medically in the right way. As grotesque as it seems today, the tendency of a certain direction is to invent means by which one inoculates children with all kinds of stuff, by which their bodily organization is so paralyzed that the materialistic mind lives quite well in them.[80]

"Phys.[ical] means against Spir.[itual]!" he wrote in a notebook.[81] As is well known, the Swabian theosophist Oetinger understood the human body as the "end of God's paths," and Rudolf Steiner, two centuries after Oetinger, contributed significantly to our ability to see and understand the body anew as the work of higher hierarchies. Parallel to this, however, is that which is pursued and decisively advanced by evil beings, which is described in the esoteric lessons of the Michael School as "consecration" of one's "own" body to the opposing powers and is brought to the point of an attack on the body, which—in the sense of Oetinger—is at the same time an attack on the entire Christ-cosmos. The "forces of the earth's depths" want to snatch the human being from the "forces of the gods," and thus alienate and, in the end, extinguish the aim and center of the working of the hierarchies; they want to get the future of the earth into their power ("...in future times seek to rob / world-being from godly being"[82]). We can perhaps claim with a certain justification that we will not allow this under any circumstances with regard to our own body, but we must admit to ourselves that conditions could develop that would limit our freedom in the future, and, moreover, we must ask ourselves self-critically as members of the Michael Movement what we can do—beyond the limits of the body—against this dangerous scenario, what concrete resistance we can offer against it. And we probably also have to ask ourselves how we treat our own corporeality concretely—whether we really do this according to the "Logos of the human physical body," in lifestyle and conduct.

All these points of view—and many more—are not only to be considered but actually *meditated* upon at the beginning, in the first third, of the Michael School, and this seems to me to be the decisive point. We can and should also think about these things, even if we generally do so far too infrequently; but here, in the Esoteric School, it is about meditating these connections—the death in thinking, which lost its spirituality, the hollowed-out soul and the self-alienated body "consecrated" to the opposing powers—to begin by meditating these things and experiencing them livingly! This is by no means easy, and it has to be endured. In the much later Fourteenth Lesson, an ahrimanic and luciferic temptation, in the false entrance into the spiritual world, in the false passage through the gate, appears once again—for the last time—as a possibility. Here the pupil is called upon to meditate not only on the Christ-impulse in his own heart, but also on the other tempter-impulses, to meditate almost *equally.* You must not, Rudolf Steiner emphasized, "shrink from it." You must bring all three possibilities "again and again" before your soul. You must actually learn to feel the inner wavering and leaning toward Lucifer and Ahriman—in order to be able to decide in the end in "free choice" for

the Christ path.[83] Dr. Steiner says this so simply, but it sig-
nifies a tremendous challenge! Can we say that we are suf-
ficiently meeting it, meditatively meeting it? It is difficult, no
doubt, but it is a real path of self-knowledge that includes
Lucifer and Ahriman—not Lucifer and Ahriman in general
and in the world but *in us*. This is what is initially frighten-
ing, but it is also precisely what aids development, in the
sense of what was said before.

"No one should shrink from it," said Rudolf Steiner.[84]
As disciples of Michael, who are or must be at the same
time also "contemporaries," we in the twenty-first century
carry the opposing powers within us ("Your epoch has
placed them in you/As enemies of knowledge..."); we also
carry doubts, hatred, and fear within us, but we should
not resign ourselves to them, neither condemn ourselves
nor surrender. The fear of one's own self (or rather, of the
shadow sides of this "self") furnishes the task of changing
this fear into "soul courage," as is stated, not by chance, in
the Sixth Lesson, which marks a transition—after all the
concentrated aspects of seduction and evil. Decisions are
necessary, but also possible, and they must be maintained
in the course of the further journey. These decisions take
place essentially in the human heart, as the actual organ
of destiny,[85] which we are reminded of once again in the
Fourteenth Lesson.

In the Karma Lectures, Rudolf Steiner said that the
Michaelic struggle, the struggle between Michael and Ahriman, would be decided in the heart. Judas was seduced by
Satan in the heart, which has a special relationship with the
higher I of humanity and is the real "Christ organ" (Jn 13:2);
but in this region, the "foundation stone laying," the laying

of the "foundation stone of good" (Sergei O. Prokofieff)[86] at the Christmas Conference, also took place.

~

What more is there to be said about the confrontation with evil in the Michael Schooling of the nineteen Lessons of the First Class in this introductory presentation? Probably still much, very much, even if after the Sixth Lesson, the powers of evil are no longer spoken of regularly in an explicit way in the mantric core of the School's teachings. You know that the Lessons move more and more into the region of the hierarchies in terms of content. It is indeed the spiritual guiding question of the whole—and it deeply concerns our ability to confront evil, our ability to limit, overcome, and redeem it: What can we human beings do to conquer the truth of our own being, how can we break through to the true core of our own being in order to withstand the obstacles and temptations from within it? What we need for this is the embracing of our total beingness in its earthly-cosmic environment—in our supporting relation to the elements of earth as well as to the moving and fixed stars in space, in spiritual space. Moreover, what is meant is the discovery and internalization of our more comprehensive I in temporal terms, of an I that stands in the present but wants to go into the future in the confrontation with many obstacles, forces, and powers, and for this needs the authority of its own past being, of its own I in this past. Commenting on a destiny-exercise in the course of the Tenth Lesson, Rudolf Steiner said:

> All that I am becomes clear to me when my past earthly existence penetrates, shines through, and weaves and quivers through the present one. For there I am. Only my present I is a becoming, is a germ, which will receive its

meaning only when I will have passed through the gate of death. That which shines into my present existence from my previous existence on earth, which weaves in, which works in, that is what makes me an existing human being, that begets me as an existing human being.[87]

In following the path of the nineteen Lessons, it becomes clearer and clearer: There are great protective and helping powers that are connected with this truth of our own being, our higher and true I; present and effective powers carry the "concern for the human world" with and within them, powers that we must learn to experience and perceive. They are present, but we have no awareness of them. We can, however, train ourselves for their present activity, we can learn to meet them *with awareness*, to confirm and affirm them in our own thinking, feeling, and willing. We can learn to live and work with them and thereby experience a considerable expansion of our being. We are not supposed to lose our "human origin" to "alien powers" but to intensify our connection with the "creating spiritual powers"—this is what esoteric training serves in the confrontation with the forces and powers of evil. The "true human I" can be grasped only "in the surroundings of the seraphim, cherubim, thrones."[88] "To let the God in the human being rule" also means to get to know the "life powers" of one's own existence more precisely and to understand and grasp the *I Am*, *I Live*, and *I Will* much more deeply than before—i.e., to arrive at what Rudolf Steiner called "the true essence of the human being." Even if in the many Lessons that form stages on this path, there is not always explicit mention of evil, it is immediately obvious that without this expansion and deepening of being, the confrontation with evil cannot be conducted positively. We must reach our true self, step by step, that dimension of our being where we are microcosm in macrocosm, Logos-bearers and thus belonging-to-Christ. To the extent that we achieve this, we not only elude the tempting powers of evil but overcome them through the "world-creating power in the spirit-I." "You do not allow the tempter to act in us beyond the capability of our strength, because in Your being no temptation can exist...."[89] "There lives the soul/That was dead/There shines the I/That was dark/There strengthens the spirit/That was closed...."

One can also say: Everything aims at a penetrating impulse of awakening—according to Rudolf Steiner—at "waking force, awakening force, invigorating fire."[90] The Michael students need a developed, schooled organ of perception for evil. Steiner (representing Michael) did not expect from us a need for social harmony, naïveté, and illusions, but a real sensitivity for destructive and abyssal forces in the world, in one's own self and in other people. He expected power of judgment and discernment from people who encountered and were connected to anthroposophy as a "gift of Michael," the "light of spiritual cognition."[91] Michaelites should be characterized by the schooled form of a spiritualized intelligence and, furthermore, by their readiness for resistance, for commitment, for the "free power" of the human heart. This is also very much about the "will-impulse" and the aforementioned "world-creating power in the spirit-I." This is to be seized, instead of the "lameness of your self," and it is to be guided consistently by our own awakened conscience—not by the collective or the norm, and also not by the anthroposophical norm or the anthroposophical collective, which very much exist: "Look at the soul-guidance of conscience." We must not collaborate with evil in any way. This was declared by the brilliant Freiburg Christian Community priest, Dr. Friedrich Doldinger, who, in view of the rise of fascism, made this clear in 1930 in his apocalyptic resistance drama—very clear indeed.[92] "*No pasarán* [They shall not pass]...."

Such discerning and resistant Michaelites as the spiritual "teacher" in Doldinger's *Wolkendurchleuchter* [Cloud illuminator] also existed years later among anthroposophists, though not too many. Two days after Adolf Hitler's first speech as German Chancellor—which he gave, introduced by Joseph Goebbels, in the Berlin Sportpalast on February 10, 1933, on the subject of his future policy—the curative educator Werner Pache wrote to Ita Wegman in Arlesheim:

> We would like to ask you once again if you would like to arrange to come via Hamborn on your way back from England to give a Class Lesson here. When I stood the night before yesterday on the Wittenbergplatz in Berlin, where, as in many other public places, Hitler's speech resounded through loudspeakers and the power of Ahriman was almost overflowing, I suddenly had a very confident, calm feeling, which was so strong that I was suddenly removed from the spell of this evil power. A feeling that our cause will not perish.

In the face of the resounding power of Ahriman, this "confidently calm feeling" that animated Werner Pache had to do with that esotericism which he asked Ita Wegman to further mediate. Wegman herself was a Michaelite of the first rank and behaved in an exemplary manner throughout the period of German National Socialism, both in her judgements and actions—exemplary in the sense of Rudolf Steiner and Michael, exemplary in the sense of the spiritual teacher in Doldinger's play. I invite you to read about this in detail in my written vindication of Ita Wegman.[93]

"A feeling that our cause will not perish...." The "cause" of Werner Pache and Ita Wegman was anthroposophical curative education and anthroposophy itself, and it indeed did not perish, even if it had to enter temporary obscurity. The Esoteric Lessons of the First Class, which Ita Wegman carried into the curative education institute of Schloss Hamborn, gave the staff inner support. They contained the source of strength for spiritual resistance, demonstrated how to recognize reality in dealing with evil, gave orientation and in a certain sense also esoteric "protection"; however, it was not about salvation, but about cooperation—cooperation in Michael's struggle with Ahriman, cooperation at Michael's side. "Michael needs hosts of helpers," Rudolf Steiner once said,[94] and I would like to add: *Because* Michael needs "hosts of helpers," he founded his School on earth in 1923/24, once the first receptive people were available (among them Ita Wegman, from whom came the question and the initiative for the establishment of the School).[95] Michael founded the School and he leads it, as Steiner repeatedly made clear— Michael, the "leader of the spiritual current of humanity in the present."[96]

Leading National Socialists, including in particular the SS leader Heinrich Himmler, attempted to work not least of all with occult methods; in this respect, too, the Michael School was and is of unique value as a counterbalance. As Rudolf Steiner repeatedly pointed out, the misuse of spiritual forces—with egoistic aims—will increase in the near future and threaten civilization, the salvation of the soul of individuals, communities, and whole societies. Here, too, the Michael School, correctly understood and applied, forms a "rock for anthroposophy"—and thus a *place of resistance*, the importance of which will certainly become far greater in the future; which is why we must also make the Michael School discoverable, accessible, without diminishing its spiritual seriousness. This resistance, however, will demand effort from the Michaelites in the age of evil, as Steiner also explicitly said in the context of the Lessons:

> We will still have quite a hard time with anthroposophy, and the members of the School must know that they will have to deal with these difficulties. They are not merely anthroposophists, they are members of an esoteric school.[97]

The members would be "tested"—Rudolf Steiner used this expression often, and he spoke of coming demands. The question of a "representation" of anthroposophy in the age of evil was not a game for Steiner but a matter of absolute seriousness, and it is, besides everything else, a question of courage. The Michael School, as an "institution of the spiritual world for the present," is necessarily placed in this present and its abysses; there is no way around it. How one can work from this school, this "heavenly institution" and its spirit in the times of evil and persecution, with the "foundation stone of good" in the heart, I ask in the chapter "Spirituality at the Abyss: Ita Wegman and the Civilizational Significance of the Michael School" in my written vindication of Ita Wegman.[98] Ita Wegman knew the human being and human beings in their "soul foundations"; she knew the forces of good *and* evil working there, and was a highly schooled soul in this respect.

~

"He will one day unite for the advancement of the world with those whom, through their bearing, he can wrest from the death of matter." These words of the Creed,[99] in my opinion, also belong here, in this context. The "death of matter" includes Ahriman's realm—souls are to be "wrested" from Ahriman, or rather: they want to find the way to Christ in Ahriman's realm with the help of Michael. They are to find themselves in the Michael School, in their true I, as was said before—the one in which they themselves are Logos-bearers and belong to the World-word. "*World is I-willing spirit-word*"—this statement, in which the schooling culminates, is the real answer to Sorat, to the Anti-Christ who fights the I-principle. Michael-Christ, however, stands for the spirit-willed I, for whose sake the earth-world exists. The way of the I and the sense for earth existence, the "earth sense," are closely connected. The Michael School and schooling, Rudolf Steiner once explicitly said, is about the "core" of a future humanity, and I think we still see it much too narrowly. *The core of a future humanity*—that is decidedly more than our internal community, our small anthroposophical flock.

I hope that with these remarks, although they have been so brief and aphoristic, the concerns of the Michael School and schooling have become somewhat clearer, if only in one respect. I hope that within this School a real spiritual community building will be possible in the future, the building of a community that we absolutely need for the great confrontation with Ahriman and the forces of evil, a community of the Foundation Stone that—in the sense of Rudolf Steiner's introductory quotation—will succeed in solving the problem of evil in a "vital way." We still often feel powerless, but it need not and cannot remain so. We have to find anew the whole strength of the School and of the schooling out of nothing and, when the old no longer suffices and Notre Dame burns, we have to build new, "spiritual cathedrals," as Peter F. Matthiessen said shortly before his surprising death.

It seems essential to me that the Esoteric Lessons really have the power of spiritual enactments, the power of a spiritual action in an esoteric community, where Michael is present with his spirit and his love ("...that Michael dwells in spirit and soul among us").[100] This is about Lessons that enable Michael to "strengthen" and "bless" that which approaches his students in "mantric thoughts." Many members have experienced such Lessons and such Class communities; around these Lessons and through the Lessons, "sheaths" are woven for the reappearance of the Christ in the etheric—besides all the other tasks connected with holding the Lessons—sheaths made of forces of wonder and awe, of compassion and love, but also of conscience. All these qualities are addressed and called upon in the Class Lessons; they are present whenever, within the Michael School, in his presence, the Lessons become "occult actions" and contribute significantly to the "spiritual strength" of the anthroposophical movement—in its confrontation with evil:

> That, then, which these Lessons contain will be the Michael message for our age. And through this fact, the anthroposophical movement will receive its real spiritual strength. For this reason, it is necessary that precisely what can be called membership in this School is taken in the very deepest seriousness.[101]

Rudolf Steiner spoke of a "School of Michael and his power."[102] The Michael School is—in precisely this sense—the "core" of the esoteric work of the Anthroposophical Society and the "soul" of the anthroposophical movement, as Rudolf Steiner emphasized in the Eighth Class Lesson on Good Friday 1924.

Likely with this background in mind, Ita Wegman wrote half a year later, on October 16, 1924, in a difficult situation at Rudolf Steiner's sickbed and shortly before Adolf Hitler's release from his Landsberg imprisonment (and his re-founding of the NSDAP):

> It is important now to bring the Michael stream forward. Just make the First Class Lessons rich in content and serious, then you will already do a good job.[103]

Michael is the "servant of the great Sun Spirit," and he "guides the future so that it becomes the present."[104] But Michael needs "courageous people, inwardly courageous people,"[105] who live "sun-guided," who recognize their own being walking on earth as "sun-guided,"[106] and who work to ensure that this spiritual "sunlight" continues to spread, despite all the opposing forces and powers. Michael relies on the fact that enough people are found who not only take part in his fight with Ahriman ("participating" and "looking into" him, as Steiner once said[107]), but cooperate in this fight with all their forces. "Demons must lose / Good primal-force beings (archai) / And world-governing powers (archangeloi) / And leaders of human beings (angeloi) / Must win...."[108]

Through the experience of evil, Rudolf Steiner explained, the etheric Christ can reappear to humanity. In the confrontation with evil, the human being can "break through to spiritual life on the level of the consciousness soul"[109]—we should never forget this. But for this we need, and for this humanity needs, anthroposophy. "It is precisely by consciously taking up, in knowledge, that spirituality to which the ahrimanic powers have no access that humanity is strengthened to face Ahriman *in the world*," wrote Steiner in the last of his *Leading Thoughts*, which appeared only posthumously.[110] We should also always remain aware of this.

~

In the last months of his active work, Rudolf Steiner further intensified the Esoteric Lessons of the Michael School. He concluded (and protected)[111] them from the end of August 1924 in a cultic way—with the "seal" and the "sign" of Michael—and he brought Ita Wegman into co-responsibility for the First Class in a ritual way at the beginning of September 1924. The ritual he performed with her could only be reconstructed and made known in 2010, one hundred years after Steiner's lectures on the reappearance of Christ in the etheric.[112] Its understanding is of great importance for Wegman's collaboration in the First Class, but also for the Class itself. At this point, I do not want to go into the whole process again[113] but would rather like to conclude these considerations with the reading of two verses, which are part of the ritual act and without doubt have to do with our topic:

Primal powers uphold me
Spirits of fire free me
Spirits of light illumine me
That I reach for spirit-existence
That I feel the soul beings
That I step over uncertainties
That I stand over abysses

In me may the Christ live
And change my breath
And warm the course of my blood
And shine on my soul being.[114]

2

The Guardian Speaks

Dear Class Members!

Rudolf Steiner once described anthroposophy as a "search for the lost word." In our time, we are searching for this "word" in a new way, and we must learn to hear it anew, must learn new "languages"—the languages of the peoples of the earth, but also the language of the spiritual world and its beings. Rudolf Steiner emphasized that the "inner" language, the "spiritual" language must be learned, experienced, known in a new and different way. It is therefore also a matter of a new sense of hearing; we are to "arouse" the "spirit's ear-power" in the "loving heart," as it says in a meditation for doctors who want to hear the word of "health" and of healing. *"May human beings hear it."*

If we progress along this path, even if only in small steps, the world begins to speak to us in a new way, especially to our hearts. Many people have experienced this on their path of study and schooling, experienced it with gratitude. There is a language of human beings but also of the whole cosmos, of the earth's periphery and the earth's depths, of the "ground of the world." What a richness! And yet it is not simply happiness. The "earnest spirit-word" is often spoken of on the path of the Michael School, and we feel this earnestness—in the world, but also in the School itself. The "spirit-word" is "earnest" and at the same time elemental. It is about the language of beings, of entities, which we can learn to hear in a new way if we want to, if we really strive toward this goal.

One must learn in an esoteric school to "listen behind the words." It is a "higher language" that resounds there—indeed, "sounds forth" from beings, as Rudolf Steiner describes, and we can learn to feel it, to sense it within, to really "hear" it. This includes the language of the spiritual hierarchies, the gods. "*I hear in the speech of the gods,*" it says in the "School for Spiritual Science" and of "spiritual development," and this language of the gods is essential—it is creative, creating. To learn it, to learn it step by step, Steiner emphasized, is of urgent importance for our further path, and also for our path after the end of our earthly biography, for the bodiless path in the spiritual world. We come then—if not sooner—into the realm of the hierarchies; we step before them, hear their speech. But whether we can then also understand this language and orient ourselves with it and by it, orient ourselves responsively in the world of the spirit, or suffer through all the "agonies of not understanding," depends on our preparation on earth. This becomes clear in the Michael School. The real self-discovery of the human being has to do with the experience of the hierarchies and their language. In one of the Class Lessons, Steiner explains:

> But the self does not stand in any relationship to an external natural being or natural process peculiar to it, but solely to that which is in the spiritual world. There are the beings of the hierarchies. If we really want to penetrate into our self, into our I, then we must not experience it together with external nature, but rather we must experience it together with the beings of the hierarchies. For

what we can address as our I from within outer nature, that is only the outer, empty reflection of the I. The true I stands in the same realm in which these beings of the higher hierarchies stand. As soon as one enters into true self-knowledge, one must enter into the ranks of the higher hierarchies. Then one must hear the speech of the higher hierarchies.[1]

Ultimately, everything is a path upon which we journey to the "lost word," a search for the "world word." It is about the language of the "world word," which, however, is a very differentiated language. True self-knowledge is not purely a turning inward but an "extensive conversation," a conversation with "World, Guardian, and Hierarchies," as Rudolf Steiner emphasized. In Friedrich Hölderlin's "Celebration of Peace," this late, fully realized poem, which was lost in the Tübingen Tower period and only resurfaced in the form of a handwritten manuscript after World War II in a London antiquarian bookshop—on what byways!—in this "Celebration of Peace," it says, "...*for we are a conversation, and we can listen to one another.*" And then, in the prospect of a bright future: "*Soon we'll be song....*"

~

Hölderlin's "soon" seems to us even today to lie in the distant future, only in the far distant future, like Mörike's country "Orplid" ("You are Orplid, my country! The distant gleaming..."). Nevertheless, it is a goal of schooling to let the spiritual world become audible and perceptible in its language, to let it speak itself. At the heart of the Esoteric Lessons are the "meditation sentences" or "mantric thoughts" spoken to us, which, if we move them in our heart, lead to inner "speech experiences." We practice letting them "resound" in us, hearing them "in soul." In one of the Lessons, we are told:

> All these words are mantric, are there for meditation, are such words which awaken from the soul the faculties through which we can approach the spiritual world, if they are able to ignite the soul.

The first being that speaks to us in the Lessons is thereby the Guardian of the Threshold, which from now on shall be the center of my contemplation. *"The Guardian speaks to the human being..."*—this is, as we know, the central content of a large portion of the Lessons and determines their progress. Rudolf Steiner emphasized "that what is said to you in these Lessons is actually the instruction of the Guardian of the Threshold himself, has arisen directly from what one can receive in conversation with the Guardian of the Threshold...." I would like to say parenthetically that behind this "one" there is without doubt also the spiritual course of Rudolf Steiner's life. The Esoteric Lessons of the First Class are built up in an objective spirit and strictly methodically; nevertheless, they have to do with Steiner's own path of cognition—they are experiences that have become objective and which are detached from him. But they were gained by what became clear to him "in conversation with the Guardian of the Threshold"; indeed, the Lessons reflect this "conversation," are this conversation, more or less. "...for we are a conversation, and we can listen to one another."

The conversation with the Guardian runs through all nineteen Class Lessons, from the beginning to the end. He is always there, the "faithful Guardian of the Threshold" who stands at the abyss of being, at the abyss of space, time, and the human heart; he never leaves us, or never completely. In the beginning, it might seem as though the first "meditative verses" or "mantric thoughts" as preparatory "cognitive moods" do not yet have much to do with him. "And then the Guardian himself speaks," so we hear with regard to the third mantra. But in the September Lessons, Rudolf Steiner then makes it quite clear that the Guardian is nevertheless involved from the very beginning—indeed, he emphasized that already the "first admonition" comes from the Guardian himself. It is *he* who addresses human beings there, who also addresses them directly in the second verse: "There you enter your own being's deep, night-enveloped, cold darkness...."

In September, Rudolf Steiner writes the first mantra on the blackboard in an unambiguous way: "The Guardian speaks," and he underlines this sentence. In the second mantra, the Guardian then essentially describes his own demeanor, his appearance, his arrival: "And out of darkness...the spirit messenger brightens for you." He speaks to the student but, at this point, of himself. I will come back to this later.

～

The conversation with the Guardian, like every real conversation, every true conversation, is an encounter between beings; we should not forget that. The Michael School is not about abstract instructions but about encounters—with the Michaelites in the community of the First Class, but especially and primarily with the beings of the spiritual world. The Class Lessons are about beingness, and they must become *being-full*, be experienced in the fullness of being; this is the characteristic style of many of Rudolf Steiner's statements. And the first being we meet on the way to the spiritual world—the world of our home, of our "origin," the world from which we come—is the Guardian. In an imaginative way, Steiner describes this in the Lesson of September 6, 1924, with the words:

> The first being that comes to meet us stands where the black, night-enveloped darkness begins. As if from a never-before-seen cloud formation, it draws itself together, becomes human-like, not permeated by heaviness but human-like. With an earnest, very earnest gaze, it meets our questioning gaze. It is the Guardian of the Threshold. [2]

He, the Guardian, appears human-like, "but mightily and gigantically formed." In the Lessons, Rudolf Steiner calls him a "messenger of the gods" or also a "guarding spiritual messenger," a "spiritual figure" who not only accompanies the events and essentially determines them through his directives, but, as such, is to be understood more and more deeply by us, by the students, as the Guardian "of whom we will hear more and more in the next lessons here, whom we want to get to know more and more precisely and exactly." A "relationship" to the spiritual world cannot occur without a sufficient understanding of the encounter with the Guardian of the Threshold. "For the spiritual world is only beyond the threshold." The encounter with the Guardian must be understood more and more: "And it depends on the understanding of this being of the Guardian of the Threshold whether one can approach the spiritual world in any form and come to an understanding of this spiritual world."

> *Know first the earnest Guardian,*
> *Who stands before the gates of spiritland....*

The "true form" and "real essence" of the Guardian
concerns us, and we, as students of Michael, must find an
orientation toward him, gain an inner relationship to him.
We are to hear him in the soul—in our soul—but in a certain way, we are also to learn to see him, to grasp him
pictorially. In various Lessons, Rudolf Steiner guides what
happens in the form of imaginative images and processes.
"We feel urged to take a few steps toward the Guardian;
we come closer to the yawning abyss of being," it says at
one point, and at another: "We have, while the Guardian
speaks these words, stepped close to the yawning abyss of
being. It goes deep down. There is no hope that we can
cross the abyss with the feet given to us by the earth." The
central event is and remains the "hearing" or inspirational
hearing of the Guardian. However, the imaginative elements are also part of the School and its schooling—and
the *intuitive* encounter with the Guardian-being becomes
more and more evident in the last third of the nineteen Lessons, his immediate standing opposite us, which we experience directly. In the essay "The Free School for Spiritual
Science" of January 20, 1924, we read:

> The "School" will lead the participant up into those
> realms of the spiritual world which cannot be revealed
> through the form of ideas. With these realms, there arises
> the necessity of finding modes of expression for imagina-
> tions, inspirations, and intuitions.[3]

~

The "conception" of the real being of the Guardian of the
Threshold depends on "whether a person can approach the
spiritual world in any form and come to understandings of
that spiritual world." He is the gate and the door, but also

the figure of light who can show and illuminate the way. Only with him and in his company do we go on. This accompaniment, however, presupposes the successful meeting of our beings, and the Guardian also speaks only "in that we meet him," as it says in the fifth Lesson. But this "speaking" of the Guardian happens in an almost bodily way. The School speaks of the word that sounds from the "mouth" of the Guardian, indeed, that comes from his "lips," and of the task of grasping his "voice." With this "voice," he frequently calls the student, allows it to "sound" to him.

"By the magic power of the voice of the Guardian," mantric words are brought forth from the spiritual world. "Mouth," "lips," "voice"—these words indicate the very concrete language of a being, language as a revelation of a being. "Let us also let the words of this spiritual messenger resound in our soul, and let the characteristics of this spiritual messenger shine before our soul's eye...." To the "characteristics" of the Guardian belong without doubt his Michaelic traits, among them his ever-present and essential earnestness. He is an "earnest spiritual messenger" with a "stern," earnest countenance and a "very earnest" gaze, a being that "admonishes to earnestness." This earnestness of the Guardian, however, is part of his Michaelic signature or characteristic: "*From his countenance rays earnestness/Earnestness, which before the mildness of Christ/Prepares the human heart for the light,*" as it says of Michael in the epistle of the renewed Christian cult. In a certain way, this sentence also describes the path of the First Class as a whole—in its own way, it prepares the human heart for the light.

Michael surges through the cosmos "with earnest mien and gesture," we read in *Anthroposophical Leading Thoughts*; Michael keeps his expression "stern," in reflection of the world's being:

> His aims are directed toward the great purposes of the cosmos; this is expressed in his mien. His will, as it approaches man, must reflect what he sees in the cosmos; and this is shown in his attitude, his gesture. Michael is earnest in all things, for earnestness, as the manifestation of a being, is a reflection of the cosmos from this being.[4]

The mien, the attitude and the gesture—everything is "earnest" with Michael. The Guardian of the Threshold, too, appears in the course of the Class Lessons not only with his earnest voice but with his earnest bearing and gesture. Sometimes he makes gestures in the course of his teachings. "The Guardian makes this sign," it is said in the Lesson of September 17, 1924—he presents the triangle to the mantric meditation sentence, "Experience the cosmic form of the head..." Much more often, however, the gestures of the Guardian are part of his intense turning toward the person on the path of schooling. About his words, it says in the Lesson of September 6: "He expresses them, the Guardian, by intensifying the earnestness of his gaze, by making it even more earnest, by stretching out his arm and hand to us in admonition." Elsewhere, too, the Guardian turns his "right hand" "admonishingly" toward us, addressing earnest questions to us, questions "that cut deeply into our souls...."

But he also uses his hand for instruction, in the direction of the spiritual world beyond the abyss, a world of spirit into which he lets us "look across" on the path—and in the Fourteenth Lesson, he even uses it for "beckoning," as an invitation to turn our consciousness back to the threshold and to him. Michael, in the cultic epistle, also performs such gestures for emphasis. In the recent past ("years ago"), he had still been spiritually perceptible, exclusively in his "severity against might of the enemy," with his hand that was "stretched threateningly toward the dragon's power." Now, however, his hand gesture turns "at moments" into "a beckoning." It is not a greeting but a beckoning to follow, a beckoning on the way to Christ and to the mystery of Golgotha, to the mystery of death and resurrection. *"Take Michael's wise beckoning,"* reads the Michael Imagination with which Rudolf Steiner concluded his last address to the members of the Anthroposophical Society on September 28, 1924. *"The protecting gods are beckoning,"* is written in one of his meditations for Ita Wegman.

~

Michael undoubtedly belongs to the "protecting gods." The protection of humanity and care for our development, the protection of the Nathan soul, the paradisal pure human being, have been among his most urgent tasks since time immemorial. In this devotion, in his sympathy, accompaniment, and support of humanity on its path of development, Michael goes far beyond other hierarchical beings, even those who are above him. Once Rudolf Steiner wrote precisely:

> The spiritual being...who from the beginning has directed his gaze toward humanity is Michael. He structures, as it were, the action of the gods in such a way that in a corner of the cosmos, humanity can exist.[5]

The "existence of humanity"—the "continuation of man's being" in the sense of the Creed—is Michael's primary concern in his communion with Christ. The Guardian of the Threshold, who bears Michaelic traits, is also first and foremost a protective figure; he stands at the abyss and protects the human being *and* the spiritual world. He knows that we can fall into the abyss and that it is possible for us to carry abyssal forces with us into the spiritual world, unlawfully, against the divine order, and thus wreak havoc. He protects humanity from the abyss and from a premature or untimely, unpurified penetration into the spiritual world—and thus at the same time protects the spiritual world itself. He is associated with humanity for its "own healing"—indeed, for its "salvation."

In a certain way, the Guardian thus also bears Raphaelic traits and is a therapeutic figure, a protective being of care, nurturing, and therapy. This concerns the wholeness, the integrity and the "healing need" of the human being. The fact that the Guardian hides the sight of the abyss from humanity for a long time is a "benefit" and is in the service of care. He knows what happens to human beings when we really set out on the path into the world of the spirit, he knows how our essential structure changes, how the soul forces dissociate at the threshold and enter into completely new relationships in their respective autonomy; also, natural forces and qualities then have a completely different effect on us—namely, as "moral powers"—light and darkness, warmth and cold, life and death. All these surprising and, in some respects, startling and dangerous changes take place in the Michael School in close proximity to the Guardian, in his sphere, company, and guidance, in "stepping up" to and before him. Then—and only then—can they take place in a healing way.

But at the moment when we undergo the shock, the sudden jolt in life which brings us into the neighborhood of the Guardian of the Threshold—at this moment we become aware of how deeply and intimately we are related to things which in our ordinary life seemed alien and external to us.[6]

We stand next to the Guardian of the Threshold. The abyss of being is there; before us—on the other side of the abyss, beyond the threshold—is the black, night-enveloped darkness; but out of the darkness there brightens something formed in a mobile way, something livingly formed. We say—feeling that our thoughts, as they were in us as physical human beings, have left us—we say to ourselves: There is our weaving, living thinking; it does not belong to us now, it belongs to the world. Light by light, the thought weaves itself free from the black darkness. We know the thought—the thought, all our thinking—is there within the black darkness as the first brightness we come to.

And then we look a little further down. We have the feeling—and the Guardian of the Threshold points us there with his admonishing gesture—we look further down: below, the darkness becomes like fire's glow. Fire, dark fire, but fire that we can feel, that we feel brightly, spreads out below. Across the abyss of being comes over that of which we know—that is our will. For the initiate gradually learns to recognize: What is it actually like when thinking passes over into willing? When thinking passes over into willing, the thought of that which is desired is grasped; but then this thought streams over into the body, streams in now—one notices it in clairvoyant feeling—like a pleasant fire. It is warmth that brings the will into existence; it is warmth, fire, as our own will which meets us out of the darkness.

And between this warmth, which streams out of our will, streams toward us—for our will, which emanates from us as human being, is only the reflex of this will, which is ours as cosmic human being, which now streams toward us over the abyss of being—between this warm out-streaming, this dark, warm out-streaming below, which has at most a bluish-violet tinge, and the bright thought-lights above: between the two there surges and weaves warmth upward, light downward. Warmth soaked in light surging upward, light warmed through in downward flow: that is our feeling.

This is a mighty picture which the Guardian of the Threshold shows us. And now we know: if we pass over from the world of the senses, from the world of physical reality in which we find ourselves between birth and death, into the world of the spirit, then we are, in thinking, feeling, and willing, no longer the unity that we are here; then we are three. In the universe, we are three: our thinking goes to the light as we cross the threshold; our willing goes to fire; to fire-borne light, light-enwoven fire goes our feeling.

We must have the courage so to expand, so to intensify this self, this I, that it holds the three together when we cross over.[7]

The Guardian is there and with us. It is he who makes the "beasts" rise from the abyss; he directs them, brings them to our view—and stands at our side; we are "beside him." He shows us the distortions and the right way, also the dangers that threaten independent thinking, feeling, and willing when entering the spiritual world. He is there and present when, in the process of schooling, the liberation of the soul-spiritual from the body begins; indeed, he has his fundamental commitment precisely at this point:

As soon as we have truly had the encounter with the Guardian of the Threshold, we experience what it means

to be with our human being in the I and astral body outside the physical body.

The Guardian, however, not only accompanies the
above-mentioned processes but also helps to accomplish
them in a very concrete way. He is a companion and a
therapist, a therapeutic companion; he knows the ways and
means to get through the existential crisis in the proper way
and helps our "true being" over the abyss. He strengthens,
encourages, and supports us to be able, in his vicinity ("near
me"), to unfold:

> But when an individual is sufficiently prepared, what hap-
> pens to him then? Then, as he comes to the abyss that
> exists between the sense-world and the spiritual world,
> the Guardian of the Threshold—if he finds him prepared
> in the way that was indicated in our previous Lessons—
> draws forth the true being of man.... Then, from the
> other side of the threshold, the first thing to happen is that
> man can behold his own being as it is in the sense-world,
> his own physical being.
>
> It is the first great impression of real knowledge, my
> dear friends, when the Guardian of the Threshold can say
> to us: Behold, on the other side you are as you outwardly
> appear in the physical world; *here, beside me, you are as
> you are according to your innermost being.*[8]

~

The Guardian works primarily through his word, through
his "content-laden, human-moving words," which mostly
appear as admonitions, earnest exhortations, or even warn-
ings—"how we should be and what we should discard." He
also poses "admonishing questions" in the second part of
the path. "But he that prophesieth speaketh unto men to

edification, and exhortation, and comfort"—Jacob and Wilhelm Grimm included this Pauline sentence from the first letter to the Corinthians in their linguistic-historical explanations of "exhortation" and "admonition." Emil Bock translated it with the words:

> He who cultivates the prophetic gift speaks to men; he gives them uplifting strength, carries the call of the Spirit to them, and encourages their souls.

The Guardian also carries the "call of the Spirit" to human beings—as well as an uplifting and encouraging force. He, too, is primarily concerned with the "betterment" of humanity, with the "purification" of the human being, with change and metamorphosis. He shows us where we stand or have arrived with our soul forces in our age of civilization, but also, and primarily, what we can do to move forward in it. He gives us clear and unambiguous "guidelines" in the form of "directives." In doing so, he first and foremost draws our attention to something. We should learn to "pay attention" to something, to see something more exactly in us, also to feel it—this has to do with self-knowledge. "*Feel how the earth's depths / Press their forces to your being / Into the members of your body....*" The Guardian asks us to experience processes in ourselves with consciousness, to examine them, but also to carry them out with greater intensity—"let rule...." The self-cognition promoted by him is a path of deepened self-awareness and a path of self-transformation; to a large extent, it is thus, at the same time, a knowledge of humanity and nature in the most differentiated way. The Guardian makes something clear to us in his teachings; he characterizes connections for us, describes them to us, "shows" them. He shows—at the abyss—the distortion or alienation of the soul forces, but also the path beyond this. He is a teacher ("explaining to us, as it were, what we are"), a teacher of human beings, in a certain sense also a "Class teacher"—and we are his "pupils," as it is also explicitly stated once in the Lessons. We can learn a lot from him about our own human being and about being human in general, even beyond the mantric verses. At one point, he says:

> O human being, by thinking, your essence is not in you, it is in the light. O human being, by feeling, your essence is not in you, it is in the warmth. O human being, by willing, your essence is not in you, it is in the air. Do not remain in yourself, O human being. Do not think that your thinking is in your head. Remember that your thinking is nothing other than your experience with the light that waves and weaves through the world. Remember that your feeling is nothing other than the general weaving and living of the warmth element taking effect in you. Remember that your willing is nothing other than the general weaving and living of the air element taking effect in you.[9]

From the Guardian of the Threshold one can learn "truths," and he promotes the maturation of Michael's students, their path to the "human self," as it is said in a September Lesson. The "admonitions" of the Guardian, however, are never imperatives; they do not exert compulsion but take place in the space of freedom. It is true that at one point it says, "you must respect the abyss," but the weight, the emphasis, is on "respect," on awareness. Only under the condition that Michael students really want to progress, "must" they respect the abyss—otherwise not. It is not a command but a necessary condition of progress that is at stake here. The Guardian always—in the Michaelic dimension of his being and his mission—works with consciousness and human freedom. His calls are all "calls of the spirit" to human consciousness. His "instructing mantric verses" address the conscious handling of soul forces, at least in the first part of the Class teachings, and they are helpful, encouraging, and "comforting" in the sense of Paul's letter. *"The Guardian instructs willing, feeling, thinking,"* Rudolf Steiner wrote of the mantric words on the blackboard during the Lesson of September 11, 1924.

~

From the beginning of the Class Lessons, the Guardian is essentially present. In the nine Lessons of the first half, before the entrance of the hierarchies, he is alone with just us, though in the face of cosmic world forces and processes. He turns to us, is our teacher, counselor, and older brother, precisely our "Guardian," and thus bears not only Michaelic traits but also those of the etheric Christ, to whom I shall return. The Tenth Lesson, the midpoint of the path, then offers a certain transition. The human I enters intensely into the events ("I live in the dark earth realm...")—going back to the starting point of the whole path—and has foresight into the realm of the highest hierarchies, the world of the gods: "I hear in the speech of the gods...." In the Tenth Lesson, the Guardian does not appear explicitly—it is not with him that we enter into a "dialogue" but with ourselves, in an inner dialogue that is objectively heard ("as if from a spirit depth," "as if you heard it, as if another being spoke to you"), and then spoken and felt. In the Eighth and Ninth Lessons of April and May, the Guardian is not specifically mentioned either, but the invitations, "admonitions," and mantras still bear his signature—and in a September Lesson, as mentioned, Rudolf Steiner made it clear that it is the Guardian who instructs and guides us here. In the wake of the Tenth Lesson, the turning point of the I and the middle of the entire event, the hierarchies then appear and increasingly become part of what takes place. They begin to speak or to speak along with, expand on, and change our previous dialogue with the Guardian and with ourselves. In the Eleventh Lesson, the third hierarchy begins to teach, more precisely, the angeloi ("in the background, the directing archangeloi")—and the theme is the connection of the human I-experience in its dimension of being, living, and acting (as "I am," "I live," and "I will") with the hierarchy's activity. It is our first "dialogue" with the cosmos on the path of the Class Lessons in which the Guardian is not mentioned. In the following Lessons, however, he enters again very decisively into events. He draws our attention to the speaking of the hierarchies, introduces them to us, so to speak—as we learn to orient ourselves on our path in the spiritual world. The Guardian introduces the hierarchies, enables us to relate to them consciously, and "admonishes" us to really hear them.

~

We are already moving in the world of spirit at this point, but are then asked by the Guardian to turn back to him—in his position at the Threshold—once again, face to face: "Then the Guardian of the Threshold calls to us to turn and face him." Although he remains at the threshold to the spiritual world, guarding the abyss, the Guardian accompanies our progress, maintains a relationship with us, and also demands this relationship ("...we are to turn around again"). The passing of the Guardian, "passing by" him cannot and must not be a "leaving behind" but must remain a dialogical relationship, an assurance and a self-examination—also in view of the fact that we as students, as long as our earthly biographies last, must return again and again from the world of the spirit into the earthly world. The "threshold" is not one to be passed once, but it must remain present, and with it the figure of the Guardian.

In the Fourteenth Lesson, the Guardian begins for the first time to ask questions—queries in a certain sense, queries to us in our changed life experience or state of being. "Where is the earth's firmness that supported you?" He asks about the conditions of our changed being in the spiritual world, about our inner attitude and inner way, which is decisive for everything else; he asks about the orientation of the heart. "There is once again the task of the Guardian...." He asks very intensely, but again not only with words but gesturally reinforced:

> So then, beyond the abyss, we feel ourselves already standing inside the spiritual world, still as if standing in utter darkness; the Guardian of the Threshold at the abyss, admonishingly staying us with his right hand, addressing questions to us that cut deeply into our souls.[10]

Now, in bodiless existence, the elements no longer fulfill their previous task—the solid earth is no longer a "support," the water no longer provides its penetrating "forming force," the air (the air's "stimulating power") no longer has an awakening effect—and also that which was previously made possible in the state of body-bound and body-borne existence by the warmth, in activating or "inflaming" the acts of the I, must now happen in other ways. "*Where is the*

earth's firmness, which supported you? Where is the water's
forming force, which penetrated you? Where is the power
of the air that awakened you? Where is the purification of
fire, which kindled the I in you?" The human heart—the
actual organ of destiny—is called upon to answer concerning the guiding principles of further inner orientation, which,
still near the threshold and its abyss, having crossed only
recently, is exceedingly embattled, as becomes clear in this
Lesson. The dramatic situation in the struggle for our human
essence and path is by no means finished with the crossing
of the abyss and its beasts. The powers standing behind the
beasts and determining them continue to work on:

> [We] must feel ourselves clearly standing beyond this
> threshold of the abyss, the admonishing Guardian of
> the Threshold at our side; within us the voices that tug
> us toward the most diverse sides: Lucifer and Ahriman;
> within us the voice of the Christ, who shows us the right
> way, in that Lucifer from one side, Ahriman from the
> other, want to mislead us.

The Guardian, however, although he does not give up
his position at the threshold and does not hurry after us,
is at our side ("beside us"). The dynamic relationship with
him, and thus also with the situation at the threshold, is preserved. The "wonderful dialogue at the threshold between
the Guardian and the human being" continues or really just
begins, in the sense of a real conversation. Furthermore, in
the following Lessons, the Guardian asks what becomes of
the elements as such—while the challenges to the human
being come increasingly from the circle of hierarchies
("sense," "experience," "look;" "recognize," "feel," "will;"
"seize," "warm," "awaken" ...).

On the first half of the path of the Class Lessons, the voice of summons and exhortation had always emanated from the Guardian, had always been his. Now, however, the hierarchies at least participate in these events—"mutual words of exhortation" are spoken to the human being, according to Rudolf Steiner, and even when the hierarchies speak, the Guardian is obviously also present and, in a certain way, also active in the vicinity of the human being. The "admonishing words arising from the communion of the Guardian of the Threshold with the hierarchies" are of outstanding importance for the further path which the Guardian accompanies, in earnest concern, in "earnest gesture extending toward us, admonishing us." This "extending" of the Guardian from the threshold toward the human being points to his continued relation to us, his intensive accompaniment.

However, the more we come into the light of the spiritual world and the lighter the new world becomes for us, the more intensively do we also seek the closeness of the Guardian in the sense of a real "dialogue," a mutual attention. In the Sixteenth Lesson, after the Guardian's question concerning the future of the warmth element, we turn for the first time independently inward toward the Guardian, "seeking help"; we seek his nearness in our orientation within the world of light, we "feel" our way toward him as the "spirit messenger":

> We feel our way toward the Guardian of the Threshold. We only really saw him while we were still on the other side, in the fields of sense. We stepped across into darkness where, to begin with, we only heard his stern and questioning word.
>
> But now, this stern and questioning word has led us to where we feel something like weaving, moving,

ever-working light—gentle, weaving light. Looking for help amid this weaving, working light, we turn to the Guardian of the Threshold. It is a strange experience: not yet light, but so that we feel that the light is present. And then, amid this light which we can only feel, the Guardian of the Threshold manifests himself again. It is as though he were now growing far more intimate with us, as though he were leaning more toward us, and as though we were also coming closer to him.

What he now says is as when in human life someone says something very quietly, confidingly into our ear. What sounded at first so clearly, resonantly—the solemn word of exhortation from the Guardian of the Threshold that sounded with might and majesty like a trumpet-call from all quarters of the cosmos deep into our heart—now continues in a tender, intimate conversation amid the weaving, working light: a conversation with the Guardian of the Threshold, for now it is as though he is no longer speaking aloud to us but is whispering into our ear: *Has your spirit understood?*[11]

Again, the Guardian inquires, but his questions address themselves for the first time in a direct way to the I of the human being—and we are asked "confidingly": "*Has your soul comprehended?*" "*Has your body experienced?*" There arises an "intimate conversation" in the "weaving, working light," in warmth and trust, a conversation conducted with "devotion." It is a new quality of encounter and of inner space—although from the beginning the Guardian turned to the human being not only sternly and admonishingly, but also "confidingly, in intimacy," as Rudolf Steiner emphasized in the Lesson of September 9, 1924. Undoubtedly, however, something has changed through our development, through our path over the abyss and our turning back to the Guardian, face to face, in "feeling our way toward" him, in the midst of the "glowing" light. There is a "longer, lingering conversation," and it produces an increasing transformation with him or Him—with a being who experiences a strong Christification, who seems to be permeated by Christ's "mildness" (*"From [Michael's] countenance rays earnestness/Earnestness, which before the mildness of Christ/Prepares the human heart for the light..."*). Michael leads to Christ, who stands and walks behind him—and the Guardian, in his capacity as "messenger of Michael," increasingly also becomes visible and experienceable as Christ's messenger and representative. "Now this Guardian transforms in the perception of the spiritual student into the Christ-figure," Rudolf Steiner emphasized in his book *An Outline of Occult Science.*[12]

~

As Sergei O. Prokofieff remarked, throughout the Lessons, the Guardian increasingly becomes a "cosmic conductor who calls forth the great, world-encompassing dialogues between the choirs of the hierarchies (up to the highest) and to whose questions the whole cosmos begins to sound in answer."[13] The Guardian makes possible—through the hierarchies—the path to the World Word, and remains our guide and companion, although he never leaves his position at the edge of the abyss. He also remains a teacher in spite of the increasing closeness and familiarity. In the Seventeenth Lesson, he still gives clear guidelines; he reminds the spirit pupil of the impression of the rainbow in the physical world and formulates instructions of what to do: "try now...." It is he who stimulates the imagination of the rainbow and gives us prompts ("let through your eyes..."), in "powerful words," as Rudolf Steiner points out. On the other hand, the hierarchies most definitely also continue to address and instruct us ("sense," "feel," etc.). They let us become witnesses of their own "heavenly conversation," and of their dialogue "in the care of the human world," and take us more and more into their sphere—in such an effective and real way that the Guardian sometimes has to protect us human beings and, as it were, keep us in touch with our continuing earthly existence:

> And it is then as if the Guardian of the Threshold gently touches us with his spiritual hands. We feel his being as if he pressed our spiritual eyes shut, we saw nothing for a moment, although only a little while ago we were in the light-filled space of the spirit. Then the word rises from within us...that seems like a memory of the world of sense from which we took our leave so that we might acquire knowledge of the spiritual world. "*I entered this world of sense, / Bearing with me thinking's heritage. / The power of a God has led me here....*"

In the penultimate Eighteenth Lesson, the Guardian no longer speaks. A dialogue between the second and third hierarchies occurs—and he silently points to them, points "up," in the light. Then, in the Nineteenth Lesson, he asks once more "from afar"—about what is thinking and "creating" in the "spirit word" and who is speaking in it. "We only hear him softly, as he now sends a last admonishing word to our spiritual ear from afar." The first hierarchy answers him. In it lives and moves the human I, which has found its being's true home. The path of the Michael School leads into the spiritual world—and into one's own I.

~

When Rudolf Steiner held the Lessons of the First Class once again in September 1924—before very many new members of the Class—they gained a further intensification. At the end of August, in London, he had begun to protect and strengthen them by a cultic conclusion, by Michaelic "seals" and "signs." In my book on the School for Spiritual Science and the Michael School (2014), I wrote:

> In a review in one of her notebooks, composed for a lecture, Ita Wegman wrote as follows of the summer of 1924 and Rudolf Steiner:
>
>> He told me [at that time] that people should now know that the Class was the Michael School in the world of spirit. He was the leader of this school, and I his helper and colleague. It was my task to protect the mantras: people must turn to me or to him if a member wished to give another the mantras. This was an esoteric act, the beginning of a newly beginning esotericism. At the same time, admission was arranged so that the prospective member would hear these words: "*This is the Michael School, which is led by me and Frau Wegman.*"
>
> In another recollection, Wegman also recorded the mode of admission to the School and its First Class—or the Michael School of the spiritual world—as introduced in September 1924:
>
>> From now on admissions took place in the studio. I had to stand next to the Doctor, and Dr. Wachsmuth led members in. Dr. Steiner asked the prospective member a few questions, and if he was admitted, Dr. Steiner spoke the following words: "If you wish to remain faithful to the Michael School, give me your

hand. Give your hand also to Frau Dr. Wegman, who
will direct the Michael School with me.

Until this time, admissions to the First Class had been
accomplished largely without such formality: following
written request to Steiner, the latter had approved (or in
some cases refused) admission. Now, however, as Wegman reported, Rudolf Steiner introduced a brief but clear
admission ritual, and obliged her to take part in this. In
a letter that referred to this retrospectively, one of the
newly admitted Class members wrote, "On September 5,
1924, Rudolf Steiner admitted me to the First Class. After
a handshake and an associated pledge of faithfulness, he
also had me give my hand to the co-leader of the Class,
Frau Dr. Wegman, who was sitting beside him." In all
Class lessons given in Dornach from September 6, 1924,
onward, Steiner emphasized Ita Wegman's special joint
responsibility for the mantras of these cultic lessons and
for the esoteric school as such.

The September sessions of the First Class were by no
means merely repeat lessons in the conventional sense, but
brought new qualities to light. Despite the new energy and
impetus that Rudolf Steiner displayed after the Christmas
Foundation Meeting, the previous months of 1924 had
certainly not been easy. Although Steiner had done all in
his power to fully realize the impulse of the Christmas
Foundation Meeting and to establish the School quickly,
Society members, including many who held positions
of responsibility within it, lagged far behind what had
actually been accomplished and the seeds that had been
planted in the joinery workshop at the turn of the year. In
1931, in a lecture in London, Ita Wegman said:

> It seemed that this [event of the Christmas Founda-
> tion Meeting] had been taken up with great enthu-
> siasm. But did people really admit it into their
> hearts? The call of the elemental spirits, invoked as

witnesses in the laying of the foundation stone, the plea "...may human beings hear it," did not achieve what they should have done; human ears remained deaf, and the elemental spirits, hopefully expectant of what might come from humankind, grew restless when insufficient response came from human beings. This is what Dr. Steiner told me. And he spoke of a promise that he had made to the world of spirit, and that he must keep if things did not change.

Rudolf Steiner spoke of these problems already in the Second Lesson, and this theme ran through the rest of the Lessons, too, in the form of introductory words and concluding comments. It even sealed the spiritual culmination of the Lessons at the end of the Nineteenth. The First Class was intended not only to establish a bedrock for anthroposophy, but its members should at least do what Steiner still found painfully lacking among many in the Anthroposophical Society, including those in positions of responsibility: understand the Christmas Foundation Meeting and draw the necessary consequences—of taking it and the whole of anthroposophy seriously, and committing themselves fully to working for it. Back in May 1924, Steiner had said in Paris, "A discrepancy exists, I have to say, between what I will and intend, what is said to members out of this will, and what members take up and understand." Of a meeting with Steiner around this same time, Friedrich Rittelmeyer wrote that he "seemed almost crushed by the failure of his adherents." "Among anthroposophists," said Steiner, "there is far too little serious regard for what actually is flowing through the anthroposophic movement...."

Steiner continued nevertheless. In the summer, on successive occasions, he elaborated further on the connections between the suprasensory Michael School and the spiritual history, the karma of the Anthroposophical

Society. In London at the end of August, for the first time, he concluded a Class ritually, using the seal and sign of Michael ("In the sign of Michael we receive what thus approaches us...") and emphasizing Ita Wegman's shared responsibility for the mantras:

> The verses and content of the Lessons can only be communicated to members of the esoteric school, thus to those who hold a blue card. Those unable to be present can receive the verses from others who were here. But in every single instance, someone who wishes to pass on the verses must ask permission for this from Dr. Wegman or me. It is part of the esoteric leadership of these Lessons that the factual reality of a request must reach us in every instance.

In September, Steiner once again emphatically accentuated the Michael dimension, power, and significance of the esoteric lessons, and indeed of the esoteric school of the Goetheanum, as if he wished to give its members one last chance to fully recognize the reality of these contexts and their connection with his accounts in the Karma Lectures, so that they might finally achieve an existential breakthrough and find the commitment to protect this spiritual initiative. He began the First Lesson in September, in Dornach, with a striking reflection on the "impulse of the Christmas Foundation Meeting and the laying of the spiritual foundation stone of the Anthroposophical Society" and the core of its esoteric activity in the esoteric school of the Goetheanum. He then passed on to a detailed account of the time spirit Michael in relation to humanity's evolutionary periods, each subject to the sway of an archangel, since Golgotha: "And so, my dear friends, let us be aware that the Michael impulses live as I have described in all that should exist in our time as spiritual activity and spiritual being." Then, with unmistakable clarity, Steiner emphasized the First Class's relation to Michael and the fact that it belonged to the Michael stream, a theme he had been speaking of very intently in karma lectures of the previous weeks, formulating the sentences we quoted earlier:

> And only then, my dear friends, do you rightly conceive of what is uttered here in this School if you are aware that only what seeks to be introduced into humanity in the presence of the Michael stream itself is spoken here. The words spoken in this School are all Michael words. All resolves of will that are willed in this School are Michael will. You are all pupils of Michael if you properly stand within this School. Only if you bear this awareness within you is it possible to sit in this School in the right way, with the right mood and outlook; to feel yourselves as a member not only of something that enters the world as earthly institution, but of something that does so as heavenly institution.

The archai Michael, he said, had not only founded the esoteric school of the Goetheanum but also inspires and leads it.[14]

Rudolf Steiner had performed a ritual with Ita Wegman at the beginning of September through which she had been accepted into co-responsibility for holding the First Class; humanity's essential encounter with the Guardian of the Threshold also experienced a further intensification in the September Lessons. In terms of world history, the ahrimanic "abyss" of humankind had moved decidedly closer in the autumn of 1924; Hitler was released prematurely from Landsberg imprisonment and re-founded the NSDAP—and many other events pointed to a dramatic development in the near future. The protection and development of the human being were urgent; they were "what Michael has to say to humanity in the present." In the September Lessons, Steiner formulated new headings of the mantras and wrote them underlined on the blackboard—with clear accentuation of the Guardian Being:

> The Guardian speaks:
> The Guardian at the abyss:
> The Guardian speaks at the edge of the abyss:
> The Guardian instructs willing, feeling, thinking:
> The Guardian at the abyss, demanding balance:
> The teaching of the Guardian:
> The Guardian with all-important earnestness:
> The Guardian speaks as if the World Word itself
>   resounds:
> The Guardian admonishes:
> The Guardian's last admonition:
> The Guardian will, in the brightening darkness, be
>   heard thus:

In a September Lesson, Steiner said:

> The verses of the Guardian of the Threshold come to you, my sisters and brothers, with the sign and seal of Michael.

There is also talk now of a "vow" to the Guardian:

> We make a kind of vow before the Guardian of the Threshold that we will let these mantras run through our souls in perpetual remembrance of his admonitions.

The "vow" before the Guardian was and is, without doubt, at the same time also valid before Michael or "Michael-Christ"—"If you want to remain faithful to the Michael School..."

~

The Guardian is in the service of humanity; he is engaged in "human soul care." This becomes more and more important, essential, and substantial in the present and near future because human beings who seek "salvation"—their wholeness and spiritual home, the world of their being— are more and more endangered on earth. Rudolf Steiner emphasized in the Fourth Class Lesson that the "whole seriousness" of what is meant by the encounter with the Guardian of the Threshold must be "constantly" before the eyes of the Michael student. The seeker of knowledge must be warned more and more by the Guardian of the Threshold, but also "raised up" ("...what the Guardian of the Threshold speaks to those whom he thus wants to raise up..."). It has to do with a re-establishment of human soul forces as a prerequisite of the true becoming of the I; thus, a turning to the world of the spirit, to the world of spiritual beings and to the world of the Christ and the Trinity. In his human-accompanying task, the Guardian is in the service of Michael, the "great guardian of all humankind," as Sergei O. Prokofieff once called him; the Guardian works in Michael's school as a "servant," as a "serving member of Michael's power" for humanity, "in Michael's name." He gives his instructions and mantric verses "on behalf of Michael," indeed, on behalf of "the best spirits, the best inhabitants of the spiritual world." The Guardian is, according to Rudolf Steiner, "Michael's governor at the threshold of spiritland," his "earnest first representative." Sometimes the language of the Guardian also has Michaelic dimensions, although he comes much closer to a human being *in persona* than the high Michaelic time-spirit. On September 17, 1924, in a description in a Class Lesson, Steiner said:

> Then the moment has come when the word of the Guardian of the Threshold resounds decisively, the word of the Guardian of the Threshold, as if it came from Michael himself, as if it came from worlds far away. After the Guardian has told us how to prepare—and we feel: such preparation must be—then, as if from Michael, as if from worlds far away, his word will sound: *"Enter / The door is open / You will become / A true human being."*

The Guardian is not Michael, and his language is not the cosmic language of Michael but that of a soul guide or "human soul caregiver" at the abyss; but he serves Michael, stands in Michael's place at the side of humanity, in his name—and through his language, Michael also resounds, or at least resounds in it ("as if from Michael..."). It is the "Christ-Michael language" of which Rudolf Steiner said in 1924 that anthroposophy wanted to speak.

In his accompaniment and guidance of human beings to the true I, in a common soul space with them, the Guardian is very close to this "Christ-Michael language"—he lives in it. With the Guardian, his accompaniment, his instructions, and his language, the reorganization of humanity's relationship to the spiritual world and to the earthly world is accomplished in the context of the struggles of the present and future. These struggles contain innumerable dangers but can nevertheless be clearly recognized and courageously endured. "For real knowledge does not come from that which today often drives people to knowledge, or of which they say that it drives them to knowledge, but only from courage, inner spiritual courage, which seizes the forces and faculties that can follow the paths that lead to true, to genuine, to light-filled spiritual knowledge."[15] He, the Guardian, stands at the gate of knowledge and life—he belongs to the "redemptive" element, in Hölderlin's sense, and carries Michaelic and Raphaelic qualities in his being. He walks with us to Emmaus, is at the side of humanity. He represents Michael, and the Christ-power lives in him, his earnestness, mildness, and love of humanity. He is friend and counselor, is close to the etheric Christ—indeed, his being is connected with Him, and he is a helper on the "Christ path."

I will to feel the being of the Christ.

~

Notes

References to Rudolf Steiner's work are according to CW (Collected Works) numbers and page numbers in the German editions. Corresponding English titles, where available, also appear the bibliography.

FACING EVIL

1   On the spiritual signature of the year 1917, see Peter Selg, *Die Gegenwart des Vergangenen. Rudolf Steiner und die Aktualität des Jahres 1917* [The presence of the past: Rudolf Steiner and the actuality of the Year 1917] (Arlesheim, 2017).

2   See CW 273, p. 95.

3   See CW 237, as well as Sergei O. Prokofieff, *The Michael-Mystery* (Wynstones, 2015) and Peter Selg, *The Destiny of the Michael Community: Foundation Stone for the Future* (SteinerBooks, 2014).

4   CW 237, p. 114.

5   CW 270a, p. 72.

6   CW 26, p. 115.

7   Ibid., p. 117.

8   CW 270a, p. 31.

9   See, e.g., Peter Selg, "Tode im Denken" [Death in thinking], in *Michael und Christus. Studien zur Anthroposophie Rudolf Steiners* [Michael and Christ: Studies in the anthroposophy of Rudolf Steiner] (Arlesheim, 2010), pp. 241ff.

10   CW 270a, p. 32.

11   CW 237, p. 114.

12   Ibid., p. 115.

13   CW 270a, p. 98.

14   Ibid., pp. 121f.

15 See Sergei O. Prokofieff, *The Encounter with Evil and Its Over-coming through Spiritual Science: With Essays on the Foundation Stone*, trans. Simon Blaxland-de Lange (Temple Lodge, 2000).

16 See Peter Longerich, *Heinrich Himmler*, trans. Jeremy Noakes and Lesley Sharpe (Oxford University, 2012).

17 CW 351, p. 47, as well as Steiner's follow-up talk with Georg Groot, in Peter Selg, *Rudolf Steiner's Foundation Stone Meditation and the Destruction of the Twentieth Century*, trans. Pauline Wehrle (Temple Lodge, 2013).

18 CW 345, p. 97.

19 Ibid., p. 107.

20 CW 346, p. 128.

21 Rendering by Jon Madsen.

22 CW 349, p. 250.

23 CW 343, p. 510.

24 Ibid., p. 466.

25 See Gerhard Kienle, *Die ungeschriebene Philosophie Jesu. Entwurf zu einer Rekonstruktion* [The unwritten philosophy of Jesus. Draft for a reconstruction], in Peter Selg, *Gerhard Kienle – Leben und Werk* [Life and work], vol. 2, *Ausgewählte Aufsätze und Vorträge* [Selected essays and lectures] (Dornach, 2003), pp. 387ff.

26 CW 343, p. 427.

27 Ibid., p. 511.

28 See Peter Selg, *The Michael School and the School of Spiritual Science*, trans. Matthew Barton (SteinerBooks, 2016), pp. 117ff.

29 CW 270a, p. 32.

30 CW 204, p. 106.

31 CW 270a, p. 116.

32 See Peter Selg, *Rudolf Steiner, Life and Work*, vol. 1, trans. Margot Saar (SteinerBooks, 2014).

33 CW 270a, p. 119.

34 Ibid., p. 44.

35 Ibid., p. 96.

36 Ibid., p. 33.

37 Ibid., p. 98.

38 Ibid., pp. 47f.

39 CW 270c, p. 161.

40 CW 270b, p. 159

41 CW 343, p. 467.

42 CW 270a, p. 9.

43 Letter to Caroline von Beulwitz, Jena, August 25, 1789, in *Schillers Werke* [Schiller's work], vol. 25, edited by Eberhard Haufe (Weimar, 1979), p. 281.

44 Letter to Christian Gottfried Körner, Jena, September 4, 1794, in *Schillers Werke* [Schiller's work], vol. 26, edited by Günter Schulz (Weimar, 1958), p. 38.

45 Friedrich Schiller, *Schillers Gespräche* [Schiller's conversations], edited by Julius Petersen (Leipzig, 1911), p. 338.

46 CW 270b, p. 159

47 CW 270a, p. 11.

48 CW 4, p. 271.

49 CW 107, pp. 148ff.

50 Ibid., pp. 242f.

51 Ibid., p. 245.

52 CW 270b, p. 159.

53 CW 343, p. 510.

54 CW 107, pp. 174f.

55 See CW 152, pp. 33ff., and Peter Selg, *The Sufferings of the Nathan Soul: Anthroposophic Christology on the Eve of World War I*, trans. Matthew Barton (SteinerBooks, 2016).

56 CW 107, pp. 174f.

57 Ibid., pp. 24ff. On Rudolf Steiner's remarks on evil in the year 1909—and the context of his descriptions—see Sergei O. Prokofieff, *Rudolf Steiner and the Masters of Esoteric Christianity* (Wynstones, 2019).

58 CW 107, p. 248

59 Ibid., pp. 248f.

60 See Sergei O. Prokofieff: *Die Erste Klasse der Michael-Schule und ihre christologischen Grundlagen* [The First Class of the Michael School and its christological foundations] (Dornach, 2009).

61 Johann Gottlieb Fichte, *Grundlage der gesamten Wissenschaftslehre als Handschrift für seine Zuhörer* [Basis of the entire doctrine of science as a manuscript for his audience] (Hamburg, 1988), pp. 195f.

62 CW 36, p. 241.

63 CW 110, p. 163.

64 CW 120, p. 216

65 CW 14, p. 371.

66 CW 120, p. 139.

67   CW 177, p. 190.

68   See Peter Selg, *Die Gegenwart des Vergangenen. Rudolf Steiner und die Aktualität des Jahres 1917* [The presence of the past. Rudolf Steiner and the actuality of the year 1917], pp. 89ff.

69   CW 72, pp. 212ff.

70   CW 177, p. 28.

71   CW 270a, p. 142.

72   Ibid., p. 19.

73   Ita Wegman, *Erinnerung an Rudolf Steiner.* [Remembrance of Rudolf Steiner], 2nd ed. (Arlesheim, 2011), p. 41.

74   CW 169, p. 43.

75   CW 202, p. 190.

76   Friedrich Schiller: "Ausgang aus dem Leben" [Exit from life], in *Sämtliche Werke* [Complete works], vol. 1, ed. Peter-André Alt, Albert Meier, and Wolfgang Riedel (Munich and Vienna, 2004), p. 243.

77   CW 343, p. 472.

78   See, among others, Peter Selg, *Die Intentionen Ita Wegmans 1925–1943, Zur Rehabilitierung Ita Wegmans.* [The intentions of Ita Wegman 1925–1943. On the rehabilitation of Ita Wegman], vol. 2 (Arlesheim, 2019).

79   On the medical-ethical and social discussion of this problem, see, among others, Giovanni Maio, Jens Clausen, Oliver Müller, eds., *Mensch ohne Mass? Reichweite und Grenze anthropologischer Argumente in der biomedizinischen Ethik* [Man without measure? Scope and limit of anthropological arguments in biomedical ethics] (Freiburg and Munich, 2008).

80   CW 174a, pp. 186f.

81   Nb 21, Rudolf Steiner Archives, Dornach.

82   CW 270a, p. 35.

83   CW 270b, p. 88.

84   Ibid.

85   See Peter Selg, "Das Herzorgan in der Bewusstseinsgeschichte. Aristotle–Thomas Aquinas–Rudolf Steiner" [The heart organ in the history of consciousness], in Christoph Rubens and Peter Selg, eds., *Das menschliche Herz. Kardiologie in der Anthroposophischen Medizin* [The human heart. Cardiology in anthroposophic medicine] (Arlesheim, 2014), pp. 31ff.

86   See Sergei O. Prokofieff, *The Encounter with Evil and Its Overcoming through Spiritual Science*, trans. Simon Blaxland-de Lange (Temple Lodge, 2000).

87   CW 270b, p. 26.

88   Ibid., p. 174.

89   CW 268, p. 341.

90   CW 270a, p. 117.

91   CW 218, p. 176.

92   See Peter Selg, ed., *Der Wolkendurchleuchter. Friedrich Dol-dingers apokalyptisches Widerstandsdrama* [The cloud illuminator. Friedrich Doldinger's apocalyptic drama of resistance] (Arlesheim, 2019).

93   See Peter Selg: *Die Intentionen Ita Wegmans 1925–1943. Zur Rehabilitierung Ita Wegmans* [The intentions of Ita Wegman 1925–1943. Toward the rehabilitation of Ita Wegman], vol. 2, pp. 137ff. (Ch. 2: "Die Erkenntnis des Bösen und der Mut zum Widerstand" [The Knowledge of evil and the courage to resist]).

94   CW 266a, p. 262.

95   See Peter Selg, *The Michael School and the School of Spiritual Science.*

96   CW 270c, p. 33.

97   CW 270a, p. 128.

98   See Peter Selg, *Die Intentionen Ita Wegmans 1925–1943*, pp. 189ff.

99   CW 343, p. 510.

100   CW 270c, p. 80.

101   Ibid., p. 125.

102   Ibid., p. 117.

103   Ita Wegman Archive, Arlesheim.

104   CW 265, p. 336.

105   CW 237, p. 136.

106   CW 26, p. 67.

107   CW 237, p. 119.

108   "Aus einer Meditation Rudolf Steiners für Ita Wegman" [From a meditation by Rudolf Steiner for Ita Wegman], in J. Emanuel Zeylmans van Emmichoven, *Die Erkraftung des Herzens. Eine Mysterienschulung der Gegenwart. Rudolf Steiners Zusammen-arbeit mit Ita Wegman* [The strengthening of the heart. A mystery schooling of the present. Rudolf Steiner's collaboration with Ita Wegman] (Arlesheim, 2015), pp. 232f.

109   CW 185, p. 111.

110   CW 26, p. 258.

111   See Thomas Meyer, "Nachwort" [Afterword], in *Der Meditations-weg der Michaelschule. Rudolf Steiners esoterisches Vermächtnis*

aus dem Jahre 1924. Ergänzungsband [The meditation path of the Michael School. Rudolf Steiner's esoteric legacy from 1924. Supplementary volume] (Basel, 2011), pp. 242ff.

112 Peter Selg, *Rudolf Steiner and Christian Rosenkreutz*, trans. Margot Saar (SteinerBooks, 2012).

113 Thomas Meyer, "Nachwort," pp. 245ff.

114 From Ita Wegman's admission ritual into shared responsibility for the Michael School. See Peter Selg, *The Michael School and the School of Spiritual Science*, trans. Matthew Barton (SteinerBooks, 2016); *Die Intentionen Ita Wegmans 1925–1943. Zur Rehabilitierung Ita Wegmans* [The intentions of Ita Wegman 1925–1943: On the rehabilitation of Ita Wegman], vol. 2 (Arlesheim, 2019), p. 196.

THE GUARDIAN SPEAKS

1   CW 270b, p. 58.

2   CW 270c, p. 18.

3   CW 260a, p. 109.

4   CW 26, p. 116.

5   Ibid, p. 88.

6   CW 270a, p. 87.

7   CW 270c, pp. 108f.

8   CW 270a, p. 132. [Emphasis added]

9   Ibid, p. 89.

10   CW 270b, p. 103.

11   Ibid, p. 125.

12   CW 13, p. 394.

13   See Sergei O. Prokofieff, *Die Erste Klasse der Michael-Schule und ihre christologischen Grundlagen* [The First Class of the Michael School and its Christological foundations] (Dornach, 2009), p. 323.

14   Peter Selg, *The Michael School and the School of Spiritual Science*, trans. Matthew Barton (SteinerBooks, 2016), pp. 76ff.

15   CW 270a, p. 13.

Bibliography

Volumes in The Collected Works (CW) of Rudolf Steiner cited in the text and notes. English titles are provided where published translations are available.

CW 4   Die Philosophie der Freiheit [in English: Intuitive Think-
          ing as a Spiritual Path (also The Philosophy of Freedom)]

CW 10   Wie erlangt man Erkenntnisse der höheren Welten? [in
          English: How to Know Higher Worlds]

CW 13   Die Geheimwissenschaft im Umriss [available in English:
          An Outline of Esoteric Science (also An Outline of Occult
          Science)]

CW 14   Vier Mysteriendramen [available in English: Four Mystery
          Dramas (also Four Modern Mystery Dramas)]

CW 26   Anthroposophische Leitsätze [available in English:
          Anthroposophical Leading Thoughts (also The Michael
          Mystery)]

CW 36   Das Goetheanumgedanke inmitten der Kulturkrisis der
          Gegenwart [The idea of the Goetheanum amid the present
          cultural crisis]

CW 40   Wahrspruchworte [available in English: Truth-Wrought-
          Words (also The Calendar of the Soul)]

CW 72   Freiheit–Unsterblichkeit–Soziales Leben
          [Freedom–immortality–social life]

CW 80   Öffentliche Vorträge in verschiedenen Städten 1922
          geplannt [Public lectures planned in various cities in 1922]

CW 81   Erneurungs-Impulse für Kultur und Wissenschaft - Ber-
          liner Hochschulkurs [available in English: Reimagining
          Academic Studies: Science, Philosophy, Education, Social
          Science, Theology, Theory of Language]

CW 82   Damit der Mensch ganz Mensch werde. Die Bedeutung
          der Anthroposophieim Geistesleben der Gegenwart

[available in English: *Becoming Fully Human: The Significance of Anthroposophy in Contemporary Spiritual Life*]

CW 107   *Geisteswissenschaftliche Menschenkunde* [available in English: *Disease, Karma, and Healing*]

CW 110   *Geistige Hierarchien und ihre Widerspiegelung in der physischen Welt. Tierkreis, Planeten, Kosmos* [available in English: *The Spiritual Hierarchies and the Physical World*]

CW 118   *Das Ereignis der Christus-Erscheinung in der ätherischen Welt* [The event of the Christ's appearance in the etheric world (partially available in *The Reappearance of Christ in the Etheric*)]

CW 120   *Die Offenbarung des Karma* [available in English: *Manifestations of Karma*]

CW 148   *Aus der Akasha Forschung: Das Fünfte Evangelium* [available in English: *The Fifth Gospel: From the Akashic Record*]

CW 152   *Vorstufen zum Mysterium von Golgatha* [in English: *Approaching the Mystery of Golgotha*]

CW 169   *Weltweisen und Ichheit* [available in English: *Toward Imagination*]

CW 174   *Zeitgeschichtliche Betrachtungen. Das Karma der Unwahrhaftigkeit – Zweiter Teil. Kosmische und Menschliche Geschichte Band V* [available in English: *The Karma of Untruthfulness*, vol. 2: *Secret Societies, the Media, and Preparations for the Great War*]

CW 177   *Die spirituellen Hintergründe der äußeren Welt. Der Sturz der Geister der Finsternis. Geistige Wesen und Ihre Wirkung, Band I* [available in English: *The Fall of the Spirits of Darkness: The Spiritual Background to the Outer World: Spiritual Beings and their Effects*]

CW 185   *Geschichtliche Symptomatologie* [available in English: *From Symptom to Reality in Modern History*]

CW 202   *Der Mensch in Zusammenhang mit dem Kosmos 2: Die Brücke zwischen der Weltgeistigkeit und dem Physischen des Menschen. Die Suche nach der neuen Isis, der göttlichen Sophia* [available partially in English: *Universal Spirituality and Human Physicality* (also: *Ancient Myths and the New Isis Mystery*)]

CW 204   *Der Mensch in Zusammenhang mit dem Kosmos 4: Perspektiven der Menschheitsentwicklung. Der materialistische Erkenntnisimpuls und die Aufgaben der*

Anthroposophie [available in English: *Materialism and the Task of Anthroposophy*]

CW 210   *Erneurungs-Impulse für Kultur und Wissenschaft – Berliner Hochschulkurs* [Renewal impulses for culture and science – Berlin university course]

CW 211   *Das Sonnenmysterium und das Mysterium von Tod und Auferstehung. Exoterisches und esoterisches Christentum* [available in English: *The Sun Mystery and the Mystery of Death and Resurrection: Exoteric and Esoteric Christianity*]

CW 212   *Menschliches Seelenleben und Geistesstreben im Zusammenhange mit Welt- und Erdentwicklung* [available in English: *Life of the Human Soul: And its Relation to World Evolution*]

CW 213   *Menschenfragen und Weltenantworten* [Human questions and world answers]

CW 214   *Das Geheimnis der Trinität: Der Mensch und sein Verhältnis zur Geisteswelt im Wandel der Zeiten* [8 of 11 lectures available in English: *The Mystery of the Trinity: Mission of the Spirit*]

CW 218   *Geistige Zusammenhänge in der Gestaltung des menschlichen Organismus* [available in English: *Spirit as Sculptor of the Human Organism* (also: *Spiritual Relations in the Human Organism*)]

CW 233   *Die Weltgeschichte in anthroposophischer Beleuchtung und als Grundlage der Erkenntnis des Menschengeistes* [available in English: *World History and the Mysteries: In the Light of Anthroposophy*]

CW 237   *Esoterische Betrachtungen karmischer Zusammenhänge, in 6 Bdn., Bd.3, Die karmischen Zusammenhänge der anthroposophischen Bewegung* [available in English: *Karmic Relationships*, vol. 3]

CW 239   *Esoterische Betrachtungen karmischer Zusammenhänge, in 6 Bdn, Bd.5* [available in English: *Karmic Relationships*, vols. 5 and 7]

CW 240   *Esoterische Betrachtungen karmischer Zusammenhänge, in 6 Bdn., Bd.6* [available in English: *Karmic Relationships*, vols. 6 and 8]

CW 255b   *Die Anthroposophie und ihre Gegner 1919–1921* [Anthroposophy and its opponents 1919–1921]

CW 259   Das Schicksalsjahr 1923 in der Geschichte der Anthroposophischen Gesellschaft [The fateful year 1923 in the
history of the Anthroposophical Society]

CW 260   Die Weihnachtstagung zur Begründung der Allgemeinen
Anthroposophischen Gesellschaft [available in English:
The Christmas Conference: For the Foundation of the
General Anthroposophical Society 1923/1924]

CW 260a Die Konstitution der Allgemeinen Anthroposophischen
Gesellschaft und der Freien Hochschule für Geisteswissen-
schaft [The Constitution of the General Anthroposophical
Society and the School for Spiritual Science]

CW 265   Zur Geschichte und aus den Inhalten der erkenntnis-
kultischen Abteilung der Esoterischen Schule 1904–1914
[available in English: Freemasonry and Ritual Work: The
Misraim Service]

CW 266/1 Aus den Inhalten der esoterischen Stunden, Gedächtnis-
aufzeichnungen von Teilnehmern. Band.1, 1904–1909 [in
English: Esoteric Lessons 1904–1909: From the Esoteric
School 1]

CW 267   Seelenübungen: Band I. Übungen mit Wort- und Sinn-
bild-Meditationen zur methodischen Entwicklung höherer
Erkenntniskräfte, 1904–1924 [available in English: Soul
Exercises: Word and Symbol Meditations]

CW 268   Mantrische Sprüche. Seelenübungen II. 1903–1925 [avail-
able in English: Mantric Sayings: Meditations 1903–1925]

CW 270   Esoterische Unterweisungen für die erste Klasse der
Freien Hochschule für Geisteswissenschaft am Goetheanum [available in English: Esoteric Lessons for the First
Class of the School of Spiritual Science at the Goetheanum (also The First Class Lessons and Mantras)]

CW 273   Geisteswissenschaftliche Erläuterungen zu Goethes
'Faust', in 2 Bdn., Bd.2, Das Faust-Problem [available in
English: Goethe's Faust in the Light of Anthroposophy:
Volume Two of Spiritual–Scientific Commentaries on
Goethe's Faust]

CW 286   Wege zu einem neuen Baustil. "Und der Bau wird
Mensch" [available in English: Architecture as a Synthesis
of the Arts]

CW 300c Konferenzen mit den Lehren der Freien Waldorfschule
1919–1924 [available in English: Faculty Meetings with
Rudolf Steiner, vol. 2]

CW 316   *Meditative Betrachtungen und Anleitungen zur Vertiefung der Heilkunst* [available in English: *Understanding Healing: Meditative Reflections on Deepening Medicine through Spiritual Science*]

CW 327   *Geisteswissenschaftliche Grundlagen zum Gedeihen der Landwirtschaft. Landwirtschaftlicher Kursus* [available in English: *Agriculture: Spiritual Foundations for the Renewal of Agriculture* (also *Agriculture Course: The Birth of the Biodynamic Method*)]

CW 337a   *Soziale Ideen–Soziale Wirklichkeit–Soziale Praxis* [Social Ideas–Social Reality–Social Practice]

CW 343   *Vorträge und Kurse über christlich-religiöses Wirken, II: Spirituelles Erkennen–Religiöses Empfinden–Kultisches Handeln* [Lectures and courses on Christian religious work, II: Spiritual recognition–religious feeling–cultic action]

CW 345   *Vorträge und Kurse über christlich-religiöses Wirken, IV: Vom Wesen des wirkenden Wortes* [Lectures and courses on Christian religious work, IV: On the nature of the effective word]

CW 346   *Vorträge und Kurse über christlich-religiöses Wirken, Bd.5, Apokalypse und Priesterwirken* [available in English: *The Book of Revelation: And the Work of the Priest*]

CW 349   *Vom Leben des Menschen und der Erde. Über das Wesen des Christentums* [available in English: *From Limestone to Lucifer... Answers to Questions*]

CW 351   *Mensch und Welt. Das Wirken des Geistes in der Natur. Über das Wesen der Bienen* [8 of the 15 lectures available in English: *Bees*]

Books by Peter Selg
in English Translation

On Rudolf Steiner's Life and Work

Edith Maryon: Rudolf Steiner and the Sculpture of Christ in Dornach (2023)

Rudolf Steiner: Life and Work (1924–1925): The Anthroposophical Society and the School for Spiritual Science, vol. 7 of 7 (2019)

Spiritual Friendship: Rudolf Steiner and Christian Morgenstern (2018)

Rudolf Steiner: Life and Work (1923): The Burning of the Goetheanum, vol. 6 of 7 (2018)

Rudolf Steiner: Life and Work (1919–1922): Social Threefolding and the Waldorf School, vol. 5 of 7 (2017)

Rudolf Steiner: Life and Work (1914–1918): The Years of World War I, vol. 4 of 7 (2016)

Rudolf Steiner: Life and Work (1900–1914): Spiritual Science and Spiritual Community, vol. 3 of 7 (2015)

Rudolf Steiner: Life and Work (1890–1900): Weimar and Berlin, vol. 2 of 7 (2014)

Rudolf Steiner: Life and Work (1861–1890): Childhood, Youth, and Study Years, vol. 1 of 7 (2014)

Rudolf Steiner and Christian Rosenkreutz (2012)

Rudolf Steiner as a Spiritual Teacher: From Recollections of Those Who Knew Him (2010)

On Christology

The Origins of the Creed of The Christian Community: Its History and Significance Today (2019)

Rudolf Steiner and The Christian Community (2018)

The Sufferings of the Nathan Soul: Anthroposophic Christology on the Eve of World War I (2016)

The Lord's Prayer and Rudolf Steiner: A Study of His Insights into the Archetypal Prayer of Christianity (2014)

The Creative Power of Anthroposophical Christology: An Outline of Occult Science – The First Goetheanum – The Fifth Gospel – The Christmas Conference (with Sergei O. Prokofieff) (2012)

Christ and the Disciples: The Destiny of an Inner Community (2012)

The Figure of Christ: Rudolf Steiner and the Spiritual Intention behind the Goetheanum's Central Work of Art (2009)

Rudolf Steiner and the Fifth Gospel: Insights into a New Understanding of the Christ Mystery (2010)

Seeing Christ in Sickness and Healing (2005)

On General Anthroposophy

The Future of Ahriman and the Awakening of Souls: The Spirit-presence of the Mystery Dramas (2022)

Maximilian Voloshin: A Russian Pacifist (2022)

The Mysteries of the Future: A Study of the Work of Sergei O. Prokofieff (2021)

The Anthroposophical Society: The Understanding and Continued Activity of the Christmas Conference, editor, with Marc Desaules (2018)

The Warmth Meditation: A Path to the Good in the Service of Healing (2016)

The Michael School: And the School of Spiritual Science (2016)

The Destiny of the Michael Community: Foundation Stone for the Future (2014)

Spiritual Resistance: Ita Wegman 1933–1935 (2014)

The Last Three Years: Ita Wegman in Ascona, 1940–1943 (2014)

From Gurs to Auschwitz: The Inner Journey of Maria Krehbiel-Darmstädter (2013)

Crisis in the Anthroposophical Society: And Pathways to the Future, with Sergei O. Prokofieff (2013)

Rudolf Steiner's Foundation Stone Meditation: And the Destruction of the Twentieth Century (2013)

The Culture of Selflessness: Rudolf Steiner, the Fifth Gospel, and the Time of Extremes (2012)

ON ANTHROPOSOPHICAL MEDICINE
AND CURATIVE EDUCATION

ON CHILD DEVELOPMENT AND WALDORF EDUCATION

Recognizing Reality: Youth Education in a Time of Global Crisis
(2022)

*The Child as a Sense Organ: An Anthroposophic Understanding of
Imitation Processes* (2017)

*I Am Different from You: How Children Experience Themselves and
the World in the Middle of Childhood* (2011)

Unbornness: Human Preexistence and the Journey toward Birth
(2010)

The Essence of Waldorf Education (2010)

The Therapeutic Eye: How Rudolf Steiner Observed Children
(2008)

*A Grand Metamorphosis: Contributions to the Spiritual–scientific
Anthropology and Education of Adolescents* (2008)

Ita Wegman Institute
for Basic Research into Anthroposophy

Pfeffinger Weg 1a, ch 4144 Arlesheim, Switzerland
www.wegmaninstitut.ch
e-mail: sekretariat@wegmaninstitut.ch

The Ita Wegman Institute for Basic Research into Anthroposophy
is a non-profit research and teaching organization. It undertakes
basic research into the lifework of Dr. Rudolf Steiner (1861–1925)
and the application of Anthroposophy in specific areas of life, especially medicine, education, and curative education. Work carried
out by the Institute is supported by a number of foundations and
organizations and an international group of friends and supporters.
The Director of the Institute is Prof. Dr. Peter Selg.